THe SUPERHEROES DEVOTIONAL FOR KIDS

60 Inspirational Readings
for Ages 8–12

ED STRAUSS

BARBOUR BOOKS
An Imprint of Barbour Publishing, Inc.

Our mission is to inspire the world with the life-changing message of the Bible.

Member of the
Evangelical Christian
Publishers Association

CONTENTS

INTRODUCTION

Tale of a True Believer

In the summer of 1962, when I was nine years old, a friend trotted up our driveway toward me in the backyard. He was holding a copy of *Amazing Fantasy* with the first Spider-Man story, and he let me read it. I still remember exactly where I was standing at the time.

I followed Spidey's adventures over the years, though I also read every Superman and Batman comic I got my hands on. I soon learned that Marvel Comics had many other superheroes, so I began buying those comicbooks too. After a while, I had no room left for clothes in my dresser. All the drawers were filled with comics. I was a real fan, what Marvel called a "True Believer."

The good news is, some of those comicbooks helped me become a Christian. Then I was a true believer for sure! If you're surprised to hear that fictional superheroes helped me find faith in God and His Son, Jesus Christ, remember that some comicbooks have good spiritual messages.

However, many others are junk. . .just like your

mother says. They show way too much violence, have unchristian values, and are a waste of time. Certain stories I read had a bad effect on me. And these days, superheroes have even more power to affect people, since they star in big-screen movies seen by hundreds of millions of people.

You might be surprised that this book even has a devotional about Deadpool. After all, isn't he a sick character? Isn't that an R-rated movie? Yes, and it's rated that way for good reason! In that devotional I explain why you simply shouldn't watch some superhero movies.

Some people wonder, "Can you find spiritual truths in *any* comicbooks and superhero movies?" Yes, indeed! But be warned, some of them have negative messages. But that shouldn't stop you from drawing lessons from *good* superhero movies.

The apostle Paul often quoted Greek poets, philosophers, and playwrights of his day to make a point. For example, Paul quoted the Cretan poet Epimenides in Titus 1:12 and referenced Epimenides and the Cilician poet Aratus in Acts 17:28. And in 1 Corinthians 15:33, he quoted a famous line from *Thais*, a comedy written by the playwright Menander. The Roman theaters of that day were like today's IMAX cinemas, and if Paul were alive, he'd probably quote from *The Man of Steel*, *The X-Men*, or *Guardians of the Galaxy*, if they helped him make a point.

That's why I wrote this devotional based on well-known superheroes and superheroines. I pray that you'll be inspired by it.

Ed Strauss

THE ONE-ABOVE-ALL
1.
GOD in the ComicBooks

God is hardly ever mentioned in the comics. Why is this? Well, most comicbook publishers aren't Christians. And while a few of the writers and artists are, they don't get to make all the decisions. Also, back in the early 1960s, the US government forbade reading the Bible and praying the Lord's Prayer in public schools. Comicbook companies, like the rest of society, followed this lead and usually didn't talk about God.

Comics did talk about ancient Egyptian, Greek, and Norse gods, because people knew those religions were just myths. That's why in 1962 Marvel published a comic about the Viking god Thor. Writers also had no problem talking about magic, and in 1963 Marvel created a magician named Dr. Strange. However, they usually didn't talk about living faiths like Judaism and Christianity.

Anytime God *was* mentioned in a comic, the writers had to really *want* to include Him. Those times were few and far between, but—especially in Marvel comics—they give a good picture of God. Of course, for the *full* picture of what He's like, you have to read the Bible. But it's amazing what you can find even in comicbooks.

In a 1968 *Fantastic Four* comic, Sue Storm's husband, Reed Richards, was in danger. Sue asked, "What can he do. . .against the all-powerful Silver Surfer?" A Watcher, an ancient wise being, said, "All-powerful? There is only one who deserves that name. And His only weapon. . .is love!"[1] This is a good description of God. The apostle John wrote, "God is love" (1 John 4:8 KJV).

In 1976, Marvel described an all-knowing, all-powerful, eternal Being who had created absolutely everything in every dimension. They called Him "The One-Above-All."[2] He was far greater than any "god" in the entire universe. Even the so-called god Thor was in awe of Him, and called Him "the Creator of all Universes."[3] Then there's a super-powerful being called the Living Tribunal. Many people thought he was a god, but he admitted he was merely "the servant of the One who is above even gods."[4]

Around the year 2000, things began to change, and some comicbook writers began mentioning Christianity. This didn't mean that they were Christians. But most people in America knew something about Jesus.

Slowly, some comics began showing superheroes praying to God, going to church, and fighting demons.

We shouldn't criticize comicbooks for not talking much about God. It's not their job to preach the Gospel. Jesus gave *that* job to Christians. But it's great when comics at least recognize that there is one true God.

THANOS

2.
The Infinity Stones

There is an all-wise, all-powerful God in Marvel's universe—and there's also a powerful evil being, a supervillain who acts just like the devil. His name is Thanos, and he's also known as the Dark Lord. Thanos's name was likely inspired by Thanatos, the Greek god of death. In fact, *Thanatos* means "death."

In the comicbooks, Mistress Death was a powerful being who thought there were too many living creatures in the universe. She wanted half of them killed. Thanos wanted to win her heart, and he knew that to do that he had to murder countless creatures. But how *could* he? Only God has that much power.

That's why Thanos was desperate to find the Infinity Stones. The Soul Gem lets its owner control all life in the universe. The Time Gem gives power over the past, present, and future and makes its wearer all-knowing. The Space Gem lets its owner exist everywhere at once. The Mind Gem lets its master read people's thoughts. The Reality Gem fulfills all its owner's wishes. The Power Gem makes its wearer all-powerful. Whoever has all six stones becomes all-powerful, all-present, and all-knowing—just like God.

In the comicbooks, Thanos collected the stones and mounted them on his gauntlet—a large armor-covered glove. Once he put the gauntlet on, making himself all-powerful, he killed half of all life in the universe. Thanos desired to be like God, he loved death, and he murdered innocent beings—just like Satan, "the god of this age" and "him who had the power of death, that is, the devil" (2 Corinthians 4:4; Hebrews 2:14 NKJV).

Isaiah declared, "How you are fallen from heaven, O shining star, son of the morning! . . . For you said to yourself, 'I will ascend to heaven and set my throne above God's stars. . . . I will climb to the highest heavens and be like the Most High'" (Isaiah 14:12–14 NLT). Ezekiel added, "Therefore I cast you. . .out of the mountain of God" (Ezekiel 28:16 NKJV).

The devil wanted to be God, but the Lord cast him out of heaven. And even though the evil one is still trying to bring death on people, Jesus, the Son of God, constantly foils his plans by saving lost souls.

There is only *one* Stone worth seeking, and it gives eternal life. Jesus said, "The kingdom of heaven is like a merchant seeking beautiful pearls, who, when he had found one pearl of great price, went and sold all that he had and bought it" (Matthew 13:45–46 NKJV). Have you found this stone?

CAPTAIN AMERICA
3.
A True Superhero

Captain America is one of the most famous super-heroes of all. His friends call him "Cap," but his actual name is Steve Rogers. He appeared in 1941 when millions of Americans were going overseas to fight the Nazis. Steve was courageous, patriotic, and unselfish. He wanted to join the army, but they refused him because he was so weak and skinny. Then a scientist, Dr. Erskine, needed someone to do tests on.

One army officer didn't think Steve was the right man even for an experiment. But then he tossed a fake grenade among some soldiers to see how they would react. They all ran, but Steve threw himself on the grenade to protect others. He was special before he ever became powerful.

They experimented on Steve and it made him tall and muscular. He became like the heroes of faith in Hebrews 11. "Their weakness was turned to strength. They became strong in battle" (Hebrews 11:34 NLT). More importantly, they were "strengthened with might by his Spirit in the inner man" (Ephesians 3:16 KJV).

God doesn't always use men with muscles. God likes helping weak people do great things, and He often refuses to use the powerful and the proud. Scripture says, "God has chosen the weak things of the world to put to shame the things which are mighty" (1 Corinthians 1:27 NKJV). When God looks for a hero, He first looks at your heart. He needs you to trust Him to work through you, but He knows you also need to be good-hearted to become great.

Captain America never became proud about his powers. When Red Skull asked him what made him so special, Cap replied, "Nothing. I'm just a kid from Brooklyn."[5]

The Lord said, "Let not the mighty man glory in his might. . .but let him who glories glory in this, that he understands and knows Me, that I am the LORD" (Jeremiah 9:23–24 NKJV). Captain America definitely knew God. When Natasha Romanoff called Thor and Loki "gods," Cap said, "There's only one God, ma'am, and I'm pretty sure he doesn't dress like that."[6] And as Steve Rogers, he went to church every Sunday.[7] He was a bold Christian.

Lots of people don't like what Captain America stands for. The villain Ultron mocked him as "God's righteous man."[8] Despite his critics, Captain America has had unselfish courage and strong Christian faith down through the years. These things make him a true hero.

They can make *you* a hero too—a boy or girl who can do not just great deeds that make headlines, but also quiet deeds of self-sacrifice every day that make a true champion.

SPIDER-MAN

4.
The Rejected Hero

Spider-Man is Marvel's best-known superhero. But he was a hero with money problems, who couldn't get a date, and who had an elderly aunt caring for him. Peter Parker was very intelligent, but weak and lonely. He was an orphan living with his uncle Ben and aunt May. Peter wanted to be accepted. He wanted to love and be loved. He liked a classmate, Mary Jane, but she was the girlfriend of a top athlete named Flash.

In the movies, Peter was bitten by a genetically altered spider—meaning that scientists had changed it into a new species. This gave Peter the powers of a spider, including super-strength. But Mary Jane loved Flash because he had a shiny new car. So Peter entered a contest to win the prize money. He wanted to buy a car too.

His uncle Ben told him that having power wasn't enough, that "with great power comes great responsibility,"[9] but Peter wouldn't listen. But after he won the contest, the manager gave him only $100. Peter was so upset that when the manager was robbed, he didn't try to stop the thief. However, things soon happened that changed Peter into a hero.

Samson in the Bible had superhuman powers as well. At first, Samson was also immature. He lived selfishly and used his power only to help himself (Judges 14:18–15:8). Are you tempted to use *your* abilities selfishly or to show off?

Peter was rejected in his personal life. And even though, as Spider-Man, he often risked his life for others, he was treated like a criminal. This was because a newspaper editor, J. J. Jameson, argued that Spider-Man was dangerous.

How could Peter stand being rejected? Because he knew that he was doing good *and* he knew he had great powers. It's the same with Christians today. "We ourselves are like fragile clay jars containing this great treasure. This makes it clear that our great power is from God, not from ourselves" (2 Corinthians 4:7 NLT). This power is the Spirit of God within you (Acts 1:8).

Remember also, Jesus Himself was rejected. Though He did nothing but good, people turned against Him. "He came to his own people, and even they rejected him" (John 1:11 NLT). Jesus was righteous, yet He was falsely accused and suffered death on a cross.

How can you stand strong when you're rejected? Keep your eyes on Jesus! He's the champion who started your faith and He will finish it. He had many enemies, but He never gave up (Hebrews 12:2-3). Don't you give up either!

IRON MAN
5.
Your Incredible Armor

Iron Man is famous for the high-tech powers his suit of armor has. The man inside the armor, Tony Stark, is a genius and a spoiled billionaire, but he has no super-powers. What makes him a superhero is his incredible armor. It transforms him into Iron Man. His armor gives him great strength, protects him from powerful punches, and is even bulletproof. The jets in his boots let him fly, and Iron Man's most famous weapons are the energy rays he fires from his hands.

In the *Avengers* movies, Iron Man often makes fun of Captain America. So Cap said, "Big man in a suit of armor. Take that off, what are you?"[10] Iron Man bragged that he was still very cool. But he later admitted that he wasn't much of a hero. He was an alcoholic and was very selfish.

Christians also have an incredible suit of armor. Paul said, "Put on all the armor that God gives you, so that you will be able to stand up against the Devil's evil tricks. . . . Stand ready. . .with righteousness as your breastplate [body armor]. . . . At all times carry faith as a shield. . . . And accept salvation as a helmet, and the word of God as the sword which the Spirit gives you" (Ephesians 6:11, 14, 16–17 GNT).

This armor is made of spiritual light and power. That's why Paul wrote, "Remove your dark deeds like dirty clothes, and put on the shining armor of right living" (Romans 13:12 NLT). Then he explained what he meant by "put on the. . .armor." He said, "Clothe yourselves with the Lord Jesus Christ, and do not think about how to gratify [give in to] the desires of the flesh" (verse 14 NIV).

Stark is sometimes unworthy of the power his armor gives him. Once while drunk, he was showing off for a group of women, blasting wine bottles and a watermelon with power bolts.[11] He was carelessly putting people in danger, so Colonel "Rhodey" Rhodes told him, "You don't deserve to wear one of these. Shut it down."[12]

Christians aren't always worthy of their armor either. Wearing "dark deeds" means following your sinful desires. On the other hand, wearing the armor of God means being "clothed with power from on high" (Luke 24:49 NIV). It means being filled with "the Holy Spirit, whom God has given to those who obey him"

(Acts 5:32 NIV). You're only wearing His spiritual armor when you love God and do your best to follow Him. You might ask, "Is it really that simple?"

Yes, it's really that simple.

HULK

6.
Calming the Monster

Have you ever seen a kid throwing a temper tantrum? You know he's old enough to know better, but there he is, yelling and screeching, and hurling things at the walls. He may not be turning green like the Hulk, but he probably is turning very red.

In the movie *The Incredible Hulk*, a scientist named Bruce Banner shot gamma rays at himself. (Hey, what could go wrong with *that*?) To his surprise, the rays changed him into a monster called the Hulk. When calm, Banner was shy and thoughtful. But every time he got mad, he turned into the green-skinned Goliath who destroyed things. This put people he loved in danger, so Banner looked for ways to control his anger.

General Ross was hunting the Hulk. So he shot gamma rays at one of his soldiers to change him into a monster called the Abomination. (An "abomination" is something very ugly and horrible.) Hulk then battled this warped creature. He was about to strangle him with a chain, but then he saw that this shocked his girlfriend, Betty. So he stopped. See? Even when he was "out of control," Hulk could *still* control his anger.

Of all the Bible heroes, Samson is most like the Hulk. God gave great power to Samson. The Bible says, "Suddenly a young lion came roaring toward him. The Spirit of the LORD came powerfully upon him so that he tore the lion apart with his bare hands" (Judges 14:5–6 NIV).

Samson often got angry with his enemies. God allowed it because He wanted to defeat the Philistines (Judges 14:4). But normally, anger *isn't* good. "Human anger does not produce the righteousness God desires" (James 1:20 NLT). The Bible says, "Stop being angry! Turn from your rage! Do not lose your temper—it only leads to harm" (Psalm 37:8 NLT).

Anger isn't always wrong, however. God Himself gets angry at times, but He loses His temper very slowly. "The LORD is compassionate and gracious, *slow to anger*" (Psalm 103:8 NIV, emphasis added). James said you should be slow to get angry (James 1:19). In other words, use self-control. Think you can't? You can! God *expects* you to.

Self-control is one of the fruits of the Spirit (Galatians 5:22–23). That means that when the Holy Spirit lives in your heart, He helps you become patient. He gives you the power to forsake anger. It won't be easy.

It takes time to bear the fruit of the Spirit. But with the Spirit's help, you *can* "get rid of all bitterness, rage, anger, harsh words, and slander" (Ephesians 4:31 NLT).

THOR

7.
Legends of Gods

The ancient Vikings worshipped gods named Odin, Thor, and Loki. These gods lived in magnificent Asgard. The Vikings created many myths about their gods' adventures, and the *Thor* movies are based on these legends.

In the first movie, three scientists were in the desert when a strange storm started. They drove into the storm to check it out. But soon they couldn't see where they were going and ran right into a muscular, blond man. Amazingly, he wasn't hurt. Then, to their surprise, he told them that he was Thor, the god of thunder.

Why did Thor end up on Earth? A short while earlier in Asgard, someone had tried to steal a great treasure. The Asgardians stopped them, but the robbers escaped. The Asgardians believed that the invaders were Frost Giants, so Thor wanted to attack them. Odin forbade it, but Thor disobeyed and headed to the frost planet where he battled the giants. Odin arrived and stopped him, then punished Thor. Odin took his power from him and sent him to Earth as a man. Natasha

Romanoff was still in awe of him though. She said, "These guys come from legend. They're basically gods."[13]

Thor's brother Loki still wanted to be worshipped. He shouted, "I am a god!" and commanded a large crowd of people to kneel before him.[14] But Odin didn't think that he or his sons were divine. Odin told Loki, "We are not gods! We're born, we live, we die, just as humans do."[15]

Thor was a likable fellow, noble and courageous. And when he learned humility and obedience, his father, Odin, allowed him back into Asgard.

As Christians, we understand that the stories of the Norse gods are only legends. But the story of Jesus' life comes directly from facts. The apostle Peter wrote, "We were not making up clever stories when we told you about the powerful coming of our Lord Jesus Christ. We saw his majestic splendor with our own eyes" (2 Peter 1:16 NLT).

Many people today say that God doesn't exist and insist that they are their *own* gods. But the Lord told the proud king of Tyre, "Will you still say before him who slays you, 'I am a god'?" (Ezekiel 28:9 NKJV). It's wise to know how weak you are. Don't get the idea that you're like a god. You must bow down to the true, all-powerful God. Whether you're small and weak or have great power, "you know that he who is both their Master and yours is in heaven, and there is no favoritism with him" (Ephesians 6:9 NIV).

BLACK WIDOW
8.
Right and Wrong

Natasha Romanoff (Black Widow) is an amazing secret agent. She was born in Russia when it was ruled by the communists. When Natasha grew up, she became a spy for her country. She was also a fantastic fighter. Once she was captured by Russian criminals who tied her to a chair to force her to answer their questions. But she was so clever, she tricked *them* into telling *their* secrets. Then she fought them all—while she was still tied to a chair! She beat them and escaped from her ropes.

One day, Natasha realized that Russia, the country she loved and served, oppressed its people. The government treated the Russian people like prisoners. So Natasha switched sides and escaped to America, a free country. There she joined the Avengers and SHIELD, a spy agency run by the American Nick Fury.

Natasha is like the Bible heroine Jael. Jael's family were friends of Canaanites who were oppressing Israel. One day, the Israelites defeated the Canaanites, but the evil general Sisera escaped. Seeing Sisera running, Jael hid him in her tent. But when he fell asleep, she hammered a tent peg through his skull (Judges 4:15–22). It was a time of war, and Jael had to trick and kill him.

Like Jael, Natasha switched sides and used deceit and violence to defeat her enemies. But Natasha went too far at times because she didn't understand the difference between right and wrong. That's why Nick Fury said, "Agent Romanoff is comfortable with everything."[16]

Natasha had grown up in a nation of atheists. The communists believed there was no God and no absolute truth. Natasha said, "The truth is a matter of circumstances. It's not all things to all people all the time."[17] She thought that it was okay to do whatever she felt was right in each situation. Many people today believe that too.

But right things are always right, and wrong things are always wrong. For example, stealing is always wrong. And Jesus is always right, and always the Savior of all people for all time (John 14:6; Hebrews 13:8). Natasha may be an amazing heroine, but she needs to learn the truth about God and His Son, Jesus.

Natasha confessed, "I've got red in my ledger. I'd like to wipe it out."[18] What she meant was that she had killed many people, and not always for a good cause.

The red in her ledger was the blood on her hands. No amount of good deeds could erase her guilt. If only she would turn to Jesus, she would learn that He has paid for all her sins.

THE AVENGERS
9.
Avengers and Defenders

The action in the movie *The Avengers* began when Thor's brother Loki wanted to rule Earth. He plotted with Thanos, the Dark Lord. Thanos told Loki to steal a powerful gem called the Space Stone and use it to open a wormhole—a hole in outer space. Then Thanos would send wicked aliens called Chitauri through the opening to conquer Earth.

Loki seized the gem and opened a hole above New York City, and Chitauri battleships began pouring down. The Avengers battled fiercely but couldn't stop them. So some Americans panicked and fired a nuclear missile to wipe out the aliens, even though it would also destroy much of the city—and all the Avengers. But Iron Man grabbed the missile and guided it through the wormhole. It exploded in outer space, destroying the Chitauri warships.

This was the first battle of the Avengers. And what *is* an avenger? It's a person who goes after a criminal to punish him.

Police have a duty to go after criminals, and soldiers have a duty to fight enemy armies. Paul said, "He is God's minister to you for good. But if you do evil, be afraid; for he does not bear the sword in vain; for he is God's minister, an avenger to execute wrath on him who practices evil" (Romans 13:4 NKJV). We need avengers. They just need to have the proper authority.

Paul also said, "Beloved, do not avenge yourselves . . .for it is written, 'Vengeance is Mine, I will repay,' says the Lord" (Romans 12:19 NKJV). Jesus said that if someone slaps you on one cheek, you can let him slap the other also (Matthew 5:39). He was saying to let *personal* offenses go. But the police and the courts still have to stop criminals and serious crimes. Remember, Jesus praised the widow who insisted to a judge, "Avenge me of [my] adversary" (Luke 18:3 KJV).

Leave avenging to those with the duty to avenge—or to God, the ultimate Avenger. But you can still be a defender. The Bible says, "Defend the weak and the fatherless; uphold the cause of the poor and the oppressed" (Psalm 82:3 NIV). Many people need a defender.

And remember that "our struggle is. . .against the rulers, against the authorities, against the powers of this dark world and against the spiritual forces of evil in the heavenly realms" (Ephesians 6:12 NIV). It's easy to see that the Chitauri are like spiritual forces of evil. Are you fighting wicked spiritual forces? Are you defending the weak? You can do this even in small ways every day.

WAR MACHINE
10.
Don't Go It Alone

Stark Industries had become very rich by creating powerful weapons for the American military. So when Tony Stark created his incredible new Iron Man armor, the US Congress tried to get him to share it with them.

Stark said, "You can forget it. I am Iron Man. The suit and I are one. . . . You can't have it."[19] He insisted that he would defend America alone. Colonel James Rhodes said, "This lone gunslinger act is unnecessary . . .you don't have to do this alone!" But Stark replied, "Sorry, pal, but Iron Man doesn't have a sidekick."[20]

One night, Stark was drunk, in his Iron Man suit, and doing dangerous stunts. Colonel Rhodes put on a spare suit of armor and ordered him to stop. Stark laughed and said, "You wanna be the War Machine, take your shot."[21] In the fight, the two men nearly destroyed Tony's mansion—and War Machine was born. After the battle, Rhodes simply flew off in the armor, and Air Force experts made changes to it. In *Avengers: Age of*

Ultron, Rhodes helped the Avengers to defeat Ultron.

Why was Tony Stark so selfish at first? He wanted to be the *one and only* Iron Man, even though it left America less protected. A whole troop of super-soldiers? Nope. Iron Man wanted to be the only hero getting *all* the credit.

A man in the early church had this attitude. John wrote that Diotrephes "loves to be the leader. . . . Not only does he refuse to welcome the traveling teachers, he also tells others not to help them" (3 John 1:9–10 NLT). Thankfully, not all Christians were like that. And not all superheroes are glory hogs. Tony Stark soon became desperate for help and was happy that War Machine was fighting beside him.

In the Bible, when General Jehu was at war with the followers of evil Ahab, he gladly let other warriors join him. "He met Jehonadab. . .and said to him, 'Is your heart right, as my heart is toward your heart?' And Jehonadab answered, 'It is.'" So Jehonadab "gave [Jehu] his hand, and he took him up to him into the chariot" (2 Kings 10:15 NKJV). Jehu was open to help. He only had one question: "Are you wholeheartedly for me, just like I am for you?" When Jehonadab assured him that he was, Jehu pulled him up into *his* war machine, his iron chariot.

May you be willing to share the credit to get a job done. As Colonel Rhodes told Tony Stark, you don't have to do things alone.

HAWKEYE

11.
Hitting the Mark

Clint Barton had no superpowers. As Hawkeye, he shot high-tech arrows with a bow, and he almost always hit what he was aiming at. Many of his arrowheads exploded when they hit their target. But Hawkeye didn't think he was much of a superhero. In the movie *Avengers: Age of Ultron*, he complained, "We're fighting an army of robots. And I have a bow and arrow."[22]

In the first Avengers movie, Thor's brother Loki was seeking the Space Stone. A scientist named Erik Selvig was experimenting on it, when it suddenly opened a wormhole, and Loki came through. A villain named Thanos had given Loki a scepter with the Mind Stone on it. This let Loki control people's thoughts. So he turned Selvig and Hawkeye into his slaves. Later, when Natasha freed them, Hawkeye wondered how many people he had hurt while under Loki's spell.

What about in real life? When someone tricks you into believing untrue things, you may wonder why God let it happen. . .but it isn't His fault. When you lust for things, you sin. When you have "itching ears," you believe lies (2 Timothy 4:3–4 NKJV). The Bible says, "Each one is tempted when he is drawn away by his own desires" (James 1:14 NKJV). You're often led astray by wanting things too much.

But it's not always your fault. Often clever deceivers work hard to lead people astray. They're very skilled in tricking people. That's why the Bible warns you to keep your eyes open. Then "we won't be tossed and blown about by every wind of new teaching. We will not be influenced when people try to trick us with lies so clever they sound like the truth" (Ephesians 4:14 NLT).

The devil often tries to lead you astray, but unlike the Mind Stone, he's not irresistible. The Bible says, "Resist the devil and he *will flee* from you" (James 4:7 NKJV, emphasis added). He sometimes tricks people and takes them prisoner to do his will, but there's always hope that they may come to their senses and escape his traps (2 Timothy 2:26).

The Bible talks about bows and arrows when it warns you about going astray. God said this about the Israelites: "Like their ancestors they were. . .as unreliable as a faulty bow" (Psalm 78:57 NIV). Like a warped bow that can't shoot straight, they missed all their targets. And the Greek word translated "sin" in Paul's letters literally means "to miss the mark."

Watch out for deceivers and manipulators! Stay on track serving God, and He will help you hit the mark and do good.

NICK FURY

12.
Hydra's Evil Plot

Nick Fury is the head of SHIELD, a spy organization protecting America and the free world. SHIELD works hard every day against the evil group Hydra. Hydra's goal is to take over the world and enslave all free peoples. In the movie *The Winter Soldier*, Fury discovered a huge Hydra plot. Fury learned that Hydra agents had secretly taken over important jobs in SHIELD. If they could destroy SHIELD, no one would be left to stop them from taking over the world.

Many Christians believe that these are the end times. If that's true, then the Antichrist's world government may soon come to power. And that means that his evil forces must already be at work behind the scenes.

Read what the Bible says about the False Prophet: "He deceived all the people who belong to this world. . . . He required everyone. . .to be given a mark on the right hand or on the forehead. And no one could buy or sell anything without that mark" (Revelation

13:14, 16–17 NLT). The world already has the technology to give people computer chips inside their bodies.

In ancient Greek myths, the Hydra was a seven-headed water dragon. Hydra in this movie is a lot like the Antichrist's forces. John wrote, "I saw a beast coming out of the sea. It had. . .seven heads" (Revelation 13:1 NIV). This seven-headed beast rising out of the sea is a *Hydra*, a water dragon.

If the Bible prophecies mean that a Hydra-like government will rule the Earth, then you can't stop it from happening. But there *is* something you *can* do. "The Holy Spirit tells us clearly that in the last times some will turn away from the true faith; they will follow. . . teachings that come from demons" (1 Timothy 4:1 NLT). Just as Hydra nearly took over SHIELD, ungodly doctrines have entered many Christians' thinking. They accept New Age teachings, sexual sins, and doctrines that let them live selfishly. But you don't need to give in to them!

Yes, some churches today teach false doctrines. But what about *you*? Paul wrote, "I fear that somehow your pure and undivided devotion to Christ will be corrupted, just as Eve was deceived by the cunning ways of the serpent" (2 Corinthians 11:3 NLT). What is pure devotion to Christ? John wrote, "This is His commandment: that we should believe on the name of His Son Jesus Christ and love one another" (1 John 3:23 NKJV).

Whether you believe we're living in the last days or not, keep your Christian faith simple. Love God with all your heart, and love your neighbor as you love yourself (Matthew 22:37–39).

FALCON

13.
Rising Up With Wings

A black superhero, Sam Wilson—the Falcon—appears in *The Winter Soldier* (2014). Falcon had no superpowers; he only had a suit that enabled him to fly. In the comicbooks, Wilson came from Harlem. His father was a Christian preacher, but when Wilson was sixteen, he turned away from his parents' faith and began a life of crime. Then he met Captain America, became the Falcon, and started life over.

In the movie *The Winter Soldier*, Wilson was already on the right path when he met Captain America. But soon Cap and Natasha were on the run from Hydra. When they found him an "Exo-7 Falcon" flight suit and wings, he joined them as a superhero.

Like Sam Wilson, many people today were raised in Christian homes and heard the Gospel, but they never received it. Jesus talked about a farmer who scattered seeds. Some fell on a footpath that had been trampled hard by many feet. The seeds just lay there. Birds flew down and ate them. Jesus explained that this was like hearts that were too hard for the truth to grow in (Matthew 13:3–4, 18–19). That's why the Bible says not to harden your heart (Hebrews 4:7).

Isaiah promised, "Those who wait on the LORD shall renew their strength; they shall mount up with wings like eagles" (Isaiah 40:31 NKJV). People have always dreamed of flying up into the heavens. That's why fans love flying superheroes so much.

The Bible describes winged beings like cherubim and seraphim and talks about women with storks' wings flying (Ezekiel 10:15–16; Isaiah 6:1–2; Zechariah 5:9). Moses even compared God to a magnificent eagle who cares for His chicks: "As an eagle stirs up its nest, hovers over its young, spreading out its wings, taking them up, carrying them on its wings, so the LORD alone led him" (Deuteronomy 32:11–12 NKJV).

God watches over you too. Even when you want to turn away from Him, like Sam Wilson did, God wants you to know that faith in Him still makes sense. Once when the apostle Paul was talking about God, a Roman named Festus said, "You are out of your mind, Paul! . . . Your great learning is driving you insane." "I am not insane," Paul answered back. "What I am saying is true and reasonable" (Acts 26:24–25 NIV).

Christianity is true and it makes sense. Some

people think you have to forget your brains and make a leap into darkness to believe in Jesus. That's not true. You just need to soften your heart and receive God's Word. Then you too can mount up with wings like eagles.

ANT-MAN

14.
The Day of Small Things

Years ago, scientist Hank Pym discovered how to shrink people to the size of ants. Then his business partner, Darren Cross, copied Pym's technology. He made his own shrinking suits and planned to sell them to Hydra. So Pym asked Scott Lang to help him stop Cross.

Lang had been in prison for taking money from a dishonest business and returning it to the people the business had cheated. Pym told him, "I've been watching you for a while, now. You're different. Now, don't let anyone tell you that you have nothing to offer."[23] But after failing to learn how to use the Ant-Man suit, Lang told Pym that he was the wrong person for the job.

Once a man named Gideon also felt like a failure. An angel told him that he was a mighty hero and that God would use him to save Israel from the Midianites. But Gideon doubted he could do that. He felt he was the least in his entire family (Judges 6:11–15).

Just like King Saul, Gideon was "little in [his] own eyes" (1 Samuel 15:17 NKJV).

God didn't give up on teaching Gideon, just as Hank Pym didn't give up training Lang. God shocked Gideon by shrinking the size of his army from 32,000 soldiers to only 300 men. And God then used this tiny band to defeat the Midianites—just as Lang and his friends, together with some flying ants, defeated Cross and the agents of Hydra. Ants were Ant-Man's helpers, and the Bible praises them, saying, "Take a lesson from the ants. . . . Learn from their ways and become wise!" (Proverbs 6:6 NLT).

The Bible asks, "Who has despised [looked down on] the day of small things?" (Zechariah 4:10 NKJV). The truth is we all have. It was easy for Gideon to doubt that he could defeat a huge army with only 300 men. After all, the Midianites were like "swarms of locusts. It was impossible to count them" (Judges 6:5 NIV).

Too often you may think you're small and hopeless. Surely God could find somebody better! But remember what God told the prophet Samuel when Samuel thought a tall, muscular man was the man God had chosen: "Do not consider his appearance or his height. . . . People look at the outward appearance, but the

LORD looks at the heart" (1 Samuel 16:7 NIV).

If you think you're a failure, think again. God has been watching you for a while, and He knows you can do things even you don't realize you can do.

VISION
15.
Who Is Worthy?

In the movie *Avengers: The Age of Ultron*, each of the Avengers tried to lift Thor's hammer, Mjölnir. No one could do it. Thor told them why: "You are not worthy."[24]

Meanwhile, Ultron, a super-intelligence that lived in one of the Infinity Stones, uploaded into a robot's body. Ultron then began fighting the Avengers. But Dr. Helen Cho created a new artificial body, powered by an Infinity Stone. Then two Avengers uploaded Jarvis into it—and the superhero Vision was born.

However, because Vision was powered by an Infinity Stone, just like Ultron, most of the Avengers didn't trust him. Vision said they *had* to trust him if they wanted to stop Ultron. He then picked up Thor's hammer, handed it to him, and said they needed to get going. He had just lifted Mjölnir! This proved Vision was *worthy* of having an Infinity Stone. Then he helped the Avengers defeat Ultron.

When you think of the words "Who is worthy?" you probably think of people who did so many good things that they were given a special honor or award.

This happened one day in heaven. When the apostle John was standing before God's throne, he saw God hold a great scroll, held shut by seven stamped lumps of hard wax. Then John heard an angel ask, "Who is worthy to open the scroll?" (Revelation 5:2 NKJV). No one in heaven or earth could. So John wept "because no one was found worthy to open and read the scroll, or to look at it" (verse 4).

Then Jesus, God's only Son, took the scroll and opened it. The twenty-four elders, who sat on thrones surrounding God, sang, "You are worthy to take the scroll, and to open its seals; for You were slain, and have redeemed us to God by Your blood." Then John heard great crowds in heaven shouting that Jesus was worthy to receive praise and honor and glory (verses 9, 12).

What does it mean that no one in all the universe is worthy of the greatest honors, except for Jesus? It means that only He is perfect. Only He can save you.

You can't save yourself, but if you're a believer, you *should* walk in Jesus' footsteps. You should seek to love and obey God like Jesus did. In *that* sense you're called to be worthy. Paul encouraged believers so that they would "walk worthy of God who calls you into His own kingdom and glory" (1 Thessalonians 2:12

NKJV). You do this by living by the power of His Spirit, being filled with His love, and looking to Him to give you wisdom.

PROFESSOR X

16.
Different from Others

Mutants have unusual powers and often look different from ordinary people. That's why many people fear them, reject them, and persecute them. Professor X (Charles Xavier) is a mutant and has a telepathic gift. This means he can read minds. He uses this ability to find and help other mutants, and he started a private school where they can study and learn to control their powers.

A violent mutant named Magneto tells mutants to fight normal people, but Xavier says to live in peace is best. If mutants do that, it will show people they have nothing to fear. After Xavier's earliest students grew up and became the X-Men, they often fought to defend society.

It's often the same with Christians. Paul wrote, "If it is possible. . .live at peace with everyone" (Romans 12:18 NIV). Peter added, "As aliens and strangers. . .keep your behavior excellent among the Gentiles, so that in the thing in which they slander you as evildoers, they may because of your good deeds. . .glorify God" (1 Peter 2:11–12 NASB).

Like the mutants, Christians are often "aliens and strangers." Their faith in Christ makes them stand out from the crowd. While most Christians in America may not be outcasts, in many other nations believers are hated and persecuted. The mutant Storm said, "We live in an age of darkness—a world full of fear, hate and intolerance."[25]

Though you probably don't have superpowers, as a believer you have God's Spirit. You're plugged in to *His* unlimited power. And He can do miracles for you. "We ourselves are like fragile clay jars containing this great treasure. This makes it clear that our great power is from God, not from ourselves" (2 Corinthians 4:7 NLT).

Jesus commanded, "Love your enemies" (Matthew 5:44 NIV). You might have difficulty doing that. In the beginning, Wolverine asked a fellow mutant, "The whole world out there is full of people who hate and fear you, and you're wasting your time trying to protect them?"[26] But you *should* love people and do good for them even if you think they don't deserve it. The Spirit of Jesus dwells in you, and He loves them. "The love of God has been poured out in our hearts by the Holy Spirit who was given to us" (Romans 5:5 NKJV).

Charles Xavier said sadly, "Magneto doesn't share my respect for mankind."[27] Indeed he didn't! Magneto said, "They no longer matter."[28] Some Christians think like Magneto. They think believers are better than the rest of the world. They believe God favors only *them*. This is wrong. God loves everyone.

JEAN GREY / DARK PHOENIX
17.
Use Self-Control

Jean Grey was a mutant, but she only seemed to have a little telepathic power. She also had a few telekinetic powers—the ability to move things with her thoughts. But the movie *X-Men: The Last Stand* showed that Jean actually had *fantastic* powers! She couldn't control all that power, so Charles Xavier put blocks in her mind. These stopped her from connecting with her destructive power and being overwhelmed.

But one day a flood was about to drown the X-Men, so Jean created a mental wall to protect them. She tried with all her might to hold the flood back, and doing this also swept away Xavier's blocks and released all her power. Jean then morphed into the Dark Phoenix.

Magneto convinced her that Xavier only wanted to control her, and told her, "You, you can do anything—*anything* you can think of."[29] The Bible says the same thing about men at the Tower of Babel: "Nothing they plan to do will be impossible for them" (Genesis 11:6 NIV). But the thing they wanted to do was prideful;

they wanted to "make a name for [themselves]" (Genesis 11:4 NIV).

Xavier asked mutants, "Will you control that power . . .or let it control you?"[30] However, Jean's power was too *strong* for her to control—so Xavier put blocks in place. Paul wrote, "I have the desire to do what is good, but I cannot carry it out. For I do not do the good I want to do, but the evil I do not want to do—this I keep on doing" (Romans 7:18–19 NIV). So God has done something to help believers also.

God knows how selfish human nature can be, so He gave us the Bible and puts it in your heart to direct you. Think on His Word and God will help you obey it. But if you willfully disobey, you'll cause great harm. When she was the out-of-control Dark Phoenix, Jean created destruction—and died herself. Solomon warned that evil people die for lack of self-control (Proverbs 5:22–23).

Magneto flattered Jean, asking, "Why would Charles want to turn this goddess into a mortal?"[31] And he told a mutant, Pyro, "You are a god among insects."[32] Wrong, wrong, wrong. No matter how powerful humans are, they're *not* gods. You have a choice: either to yield to God or to insist on your own will. Don't yield to selfish thoughts. Trust God to keep you faithful. He will guard you.

STORM
18.
Power at Your Command

One of the most amazing mutants is Ororo Munroe, also called Storm. She can cause thunderstorms, lightning, tornadoes, blizzards, fog, and clear skies. She can also make the wind blow so strong that it lifts her into the air, while dark clouds swirl and lightning bolts flash.

Really though, only God has that kind of power over the weather. "This is what the Sovereign Lord says: 'In my anger I will send a strong wind, pouring rain, and hailstones'" (Ezekiel 13:13 GNT). "With flashes of lightning he sent them running" (Psalm 18:14 GNT).

God's Son also has authority over the weather. Once, Jesus and His disciples were crossing the Sea of Galilee when a fierce storm began. Jesus rebuked the wind, and it instantly stopped. The disciples asked each other, "Who is this man? . . . Even the wind and waves obey him!" (Mark 4:41 NLT).

God promises to let His end-time prophets control the weather also. He says, "'I will give power to my two witnesses'. . . . These have power. . .so that no rain falls in the days of their prophecy" (Revelation 11:3, 6 NKJV). Perhaps you desire power like that—not just to change the weather, but to make all kinds of things happen. Perhaps you dislike asking God to do something then having to leave the decision in His hands. You'd rather He answered your prayers exactly as you asked Him to. You wish you could simply pray and get answers instantly. . .not just once in a while, but all the time.

But that's *not* usually the way prayer works. The Bible tells you to make your prayer requests boldly before God's throne—but they're still requests, not demands. God isn't a genie in a lamp who's at your command. God is the One who rules. Even the prophet Elijah had to pray desperately for God to change the weather, and he had to repeat his prayer seven times (1 Kings 18:42–44; James 5:16–18).

Many times when God takes time answering prayer, some Christians become discouraged. They complain that prayer doesn't work. They then take matters into their own hands to try to make things happen. Magneto was like that. He said, "God works too slow."[33] Abraham once had that attitude. He got tired of waiting for God to give him a son. So he took Hagar as a second wife, and she gave birth to Ishmael—who wasn't God's choice! (See Genesis 16 for the whole story.)

God has reasons for taking His time. You simply have to learn to wait for Him and to trust Him to answer prayer in *His* way and on *His* schedule.

WOLVERINE

19.
A Changed Man

A wolverine is a fierce animal of the northern forests. One of the most famous X-Men goes by the name Wolverine, but he's also known as Logan. His most astonishing power is his ability to heal from any wound. Wolverine also has super-hard, razor-sharp metal claws. Scientists working for William Stryker placed them in him, and they're deadly weapons.

A *hero* is a noble, unselfish person who does brave deeds—often at the cost of his own life. Wolverine definitely had courage, but at first he wasn't very noble. He was a selfish slob who didn't care about others.

Wolverine is like the Bible character Jehu. Long ago, the king of Israel, Joram, worshipped the demon-god Baal and murdered God's prophets. One of the prophets who survived ordered General Jehu to execute Joram and his family and to become the new king.

Jehu was a bold warrior. He immediately leaped into his chariot and raced to the palace. A lookout saw him coming and shouted that he was driving his chariot like a madman, just like Jehu! Joram drove out to meet him, and Jehu shot an arrow through him. Jehu then wiped out Joram's family—and every priest of Baal. Jehu was so violent, it's hard to think of him as a hero, but it took a man like him to get rid of Baal worship (2 Kings 9:1–10:28).

William Stryker mocked Wolverine, saying, "People don't change, Wolverine. You were an animal then, and you're an animal now."[34] But this wasn't true. At first, he *was* like an animal. When Rogue saw the messy trailer he lived in, she was shocked.

And when Wolverine refused to help her, Rogue asked, "Where am I supposed to go?" He replied, "I don't know." Rogue asked, "You don't know, or you don't care?" Wolverine said, "Pick one."[35] Wolverine had a change of heart, however. Later, he gently told her, "C'mon, I'll take care of you."[36]

His sacrificial love came to full bloom in the end. Logan had been warned that he'd die if he tried to save Rogue, but he chose to do it anyway; he chose to send healing into her body. The wounds opening on his body and blood pouring down was very much like Jesus dying on the cross. The Bible says, "Greater love has no one than this, than to lay down one's life for his friends" (John 15:13 NKJV).

Stryker was wrong. People *do* change—and there's hope that anyone can change. Don't give up that hope, no matter how selfish or terrible you've been. Jesus changes lives, and He can change you.

MYSTIQUE
20.
Being a Copycat

Mystique is a shape-shifter, which means she can change to look exactly like another person. She imitates that person so well that she fools nearly everyone. But she normally looks like a blue, scaly skinned woman with yellow eyes.

When Mystique was young, she was unhappy with how she looked. But Magneto told her that she was perfect as she was in all her mutant glory. Mystique was won over by his flattery and became his follower. One day, after many years of serving him, Mystique lost her mutant powers. Magneto then deserted her, saying, "I'm sorry, my dear. You're not one of us anymore."[37]

There were shape-shifters in the Bible also. When his older brother Esau was out hunting food for their father, Isaac, Jacob disguised himself as Esau. Then he went into Isaac's tent and tricked his father into giving him Esau's blessing. Isaac was blind, and since Esau was hairy, Jacob had tied goatskins to his arms. Isaac felt Jacob's arm and believed it was Esau (Genesis 27:1–35).

A man named Laban then tricked Jacob. When his younger daughter Rachel was about to go into her wedding tent, Laban sent in his older daughter Leah instead. Jacob couldn't see in the dark tent, so he thought he was marrying Rachel. The next morning, however, he realized he had married Leah (Genesis 29:21–30).

Other people *actually* changed how they looked. After His resurrection, Jesus changed what He looked like so He could talk with two disciples without them recognizing Him. "He appeared in a different form to two of them" (Mark 16:12 NASB). The angels of God can do this too, which is why the Bible says, "Remember to welcome strangers in your homes. There were some who did that and welcomed angels without knowing it" (Hebrews 13:2 GNT). But beware. Evil angels can also do this (2 Corinthians 11:14).

Many kids today are copycats. They want to be accepted by a certain group, so they dress *exactly* like those kids. They wear the same kind of shoes, cut their hair the same way. . . . Changing how you look isn't wrong. Fitting in is okay. It's bad only if you're so desperate to be accepted that you fail to speak up for the truth. If you do speak out, some of your so-called friends may turn away from you and say, "Sorry. You're not one of us anymore."

If your friends reject you because you're not willing to compromise and do something wrong, know this: God will always love you and will never forsake you (Hebrews 13:5).

NIGHTCRAWLER

21.
Escaping in a Heartbeat

The movie *X-Men United* opens with a strange blue mutant appearing, vanishing, and reappearing. Kurt Wagner (Nightcrawler) has a pointed tail and is covered with tattoos. He made it past White House security but was shot and wounded just before he killed the president. Then he vanished. Charles Xavier, however, was able to use his powers to track where he went.

Two X-Men found Nightcrawler and persuaded him to come with them. It turns out that he wasn't dangerous. William Stryker had drugged him then sent him to kill the president. He wanted to make Americans *think* mutants were dangerous.

Once free of Stryker's control, Nightcrawler joined the X-Men and was a huge help. When a missile blew open the X-Jet and Rogue was sucked out, Nightcrawler teleported to her in midair, grabbed her, then teleported back to the jet. In the end of the movie, he took Storm through a solid metal wall to rescue Charles Xavier.

Is teleportation real? Yes, it is. Men of God sometimes traveled from one place to another instantly. A Christian named Philip was on the Gaza Road. Then the Bible states that "the Spirit of the Lord caught Philip away" and "Philip was found at Azotus" (Acts 8:39–40 NKJV). Azotus was over *ten miles away*!

People also believed that Elijah teleported. When Elijah returned to Israel, he instructed Obadiah to tell the king that he was back. But Obadiah objected, "As soon as I am gone from you. . .the Spirit of the LORD will carry you to a place I do not know" (1 Kings 18:12 NKJV).

And here's something else: in the movie, Nightcrawler quoted the Lord's Prayer when he was troubled, and later he recited Psalm 23. When Storm told him that anger can help people survive, he replied, "So can faith."[38] Sometimes even very odd people are, in fact, believers.

But why does teleporting appeal to people? Because they often need to escape danger. David said, "I wish I had wings like a dove. I would fly away and find rest. I would fly far away. . . . I would hurry and find myself a shelter from. . .the storm" (Psalm 55:6–8 GNT). God has provided a shelter for His children, but it's not far away, and you don't need wings or teleporting powers to get there. God Himself is your refuge. He is very near to you. "The LORD also will be a refuge for the oppressed, a refuge in times of trouble" (Psalm 9:9 NKJV). You can be safe in His presence in a heartbeat—not by teleporting, but by praying.

MAGNETO

22.
The Mark of the Beast

In the movie *X-Men: The Last Stand*, scientists developed a drug that gets rid of mutants' powers. They then offered this cure for free. Some mutants were glad to get rid of the strange powers that made them different from normal people. Others, like Magneto, said it was a plot to wipe them out. A mutant leader argued that they were free to *choose* the cure—or to *not* choose it. No one was forcing them. No one was out to destroy them. Magneto warned, "You go on with your lives, ignoring the signs all around you. And then, one day. . .they come for you."[39]

In the first *X-Men* movie, a senator demanded that all mutants register with the government. This meant telling the authorities that they were mutants and letting them know where they lived. Magneto warned, "Let them pass that law, and they'll have you in chains with a number burned into your forehead!"[40] Magneto's warning is very similar to the Bible's words— "a mark on their right hands or on their foreheads" (Revelation 13:16 NIV).

Many Christians today believe these are the end times. They think that one day soon Christians will be commanded to receive the Mark of the Beast and deny Christ (Matthew 24:9–12). John said the Antichrist's government "forced all people. . .to receive a mark on their right hands or on their foreheads, so that they could not buy or sell unless they had the mark" (Revelation 13:16–17 NIV).

When you think of how bad the world's becoming, it's easy to believe that a powerful, evil leader will take over and rule the entire planet. But some Christians get so worried about this that they quit their jobs and flee to a cabin in the woods. If you do that, you won't focus on your education or career—and that would be a mistake.

Millions of Christians in China don't really *care* if it's the end times or not. Why? Because even without the Antichrist or the Mark of the Beast, they're *already* being persecuted. They must choose to stand strong for Jesus right now. And in the meantime, they keep going to school and keep working at their jobs. This is a good example to follow.

Jesus said, "Occupy till I come" (Luke 19:13 KJV). To "occupy" means stay right where you are and plan on being there for a while—and keep busy studying, working, and living as a Christian. You simply can't worry that the end time is going to happen tomorrow. You wouldn't get anything done. Just do your best to live for Jesus today.

CAPTAIN AMERICA
23.
Superheroes or Vigilantes?

Remember the devotion "Avengers and Defenders"? That showed that it's right for police, military, and courts of law to avenge people. They have the authority. But the average Joe on the street doesn't. Even if a spider bites him and gives him amazing powers, he still doesn't have the right to attack criminals, to punch them again and again, or to kill them.

In one movie, the Avengers attacked a Hydra base in the nation of Sokovia. There they caused great damage, and many innocent people died. Nick Fury, head of SHIELD, had given the Avengers permission to fight. But now people questioned if that was a good idea.

In *Captain America: Civil War*, General Ross told Captain America, "While a great many people see you as a hero, there are some who prefer the word *vigilante*."[41] A vigilante is a citizen who fights criminals without legal authority. Many superheroes have indeed acted like vigilantes. Have you ever thought when watching a superhero kill an enemy that there's *no way* they would get away with that in real life?

You may think, "It's *just* a movie! Let them kill a few bad guys!" But the fact is, this is a big problem in movies, and it's good that people are realizing it. In the past, heroes in comicbooks and movies didn't kill villains. They simply knocked them out then handed them over to the police. When villains like Green Goblin died, it was by accident.

But things began to change. In the movie *Batman Begins*, Batman was battling the villain Ra's al Ghul on top of a speeding train. Just before it exploded, Batman said, "I won't kill you. . .but I don't have to save you."[42] He then leaped to safety, leaving Ghul to die. Most fans didn't care. After all, Ghul "deserved" to die. But that started Batman down a dark path: a few years later he made a Kryptonite spear to stab Superman in the heart.

We must obey the laws, and here's one Bible law: "You shall not murder" (Exodus 20:13 NIV). King David is an example of the attitude you should have. God promised David that he'd be the king of Israel, so insane King Saul began hunting him. Saul soon murdered many people. David twice had a chance to kill Saul, but he refused to (1 Samuel 24, 26).

You may also be tempted to take matters into your own hands, to "even the score" with your enemies. But you do well to leave justice in the hands of God and the police.

SPIDER-MAN

24.
The Power of Forgiveness

In *Spider-Man 3*, Peter Parker was in Central Park when a meteorite fell. An alien being shaped like liquid tar came out of the meteorite and attached to him. It was a Symbiote, a parasite that took over people's minds. But it could only do so if the person gave in to dark emotions.

Not long after, Peter heard that his uncle Ben's killer, Flint Marko, had escaped prison. Peter wanted revenge, and this opened the door for the Symbiote. Soon—as Spider-Man—Peter felt greater power, but he was also aggressive and selfish. When Peter learned that a photographer named Edward Brock had changed photos of Spider-Man to make him look like a villain, Peter accused him. Brock begged for mercy, but Peter reported him to the newspaper anyway, and Brock was fired.

Peter's aunt May was a Christian, and when Peter told her that he wanted revenge on Marko, she said, "It's like a poison. It can take you over. Before you know it, turn us into something ugly."[43] But Peter's mind was made up.

After he accidentally hit Mary Jane, Peter realized he had changed for the worse. In his Spider-Man costume, he climbed up a church bell tower, desperate to be free from the Symbiote. But it was too strong. Then the ringing of the church bells weakened it, it lost its grip, and Peter ripped it from his body and cast it away.

Meanwhile, Brock was in the church below, where he prayed for God to kill Peter Parker. The Symbiote fell on Brock and changed him into the villain Venom. Peter then fought Venom and eventually defeated him.

Peter had learned his lesson on forgiveness. In the end of the movie when Flint Marko told him he was sorry for killing his uncle, Peter forgave him. This message is Christian, since forgiveness is at the heart of Jesus' teaching. The Bible says, "Be kind and tenderhearted to one another, and forgive one another, as God has forgiven you through Christ" (Ephesians 4:32 GNT). God knows that it's wrong when someone deliberately hurts you. He knows you'll be tempted to hurt that person in return.

But only God can judge perfectly. So the Bible says, "Do not take revenge. . .for it is written: 'It is mine to avenge; I will repay,' says the Lord" (Romans 12:19

NIV). It takes faith to trust God to make things right. You must let go of the offense and give Him room to work. He wants you to forgive the person who hurt you. After all, God forgives you. . .*if* you forgive others (Matthew 6:15).

MR. FANTASTIC
25.
Men of Great Wisdom

In the first *Fantastic Four* movie (2005), Reed Richards discovered that a powerful cosmic energy storm was going to pass by Earth. Reed thought that such energy storms had caused rapid changes to life on Earth in the past. He wanted to place some bacteria in the path of the storm to see what changes it made. So he talked Victor von Doom into taking him to his private space station.

Reed Richards, Susan and Johnny Storm, Ben Grimm, and Victor von Doom flew up. But the cosmic storm arrived early. They weren't protected and were exposed to it. *They* became the experiment! And the cosmic energy made huge, sudden changes to them. Reed (later called Mr. Fantastic) could stretch his body into any shape he wished.

Reed was also known for working too hard. Once he began doing something, he became so focused that he blocked out everyone. He had no time for friends. When he asked why there were so many strangers at his bachelor party, Johnny answered, "I would have invited some of your friends, but you don't have any."[44]

One time, Reed told Johnny that he needed to think before he acted. Johnny replied, "Yeah, but you see. . . you always think, you never act!"[45] Reed certainly *did* think. He was the brains of the Fantastic Four.

There were extremely smart men in the Bible also. King Solomon was the wisest man who ever lived, but King Uzziah was the most famous inventor. He created machines to mount on city walls so soldiers could shoot arrows and hurl large stones at enemy armies (2 Chronicles 26:15). There was once a wise man who saved his city by his great wisdom. But later nobody even remembered his name (Ecclesiastes 9:15). Even so, Solomon said, "Wisdom is better than strength" (Ecclesiastes 9:16 NIV). In the comics, again and again, Reed saved the day with his smarts too.

God said, "Let not the wise boast of their wisdom . . .but let the one who boasts boast about this: that they have the understanding to know me, that I am the LORD" (Jeremiah 9:23–24 NIV). It *is* good to have knowledge and wisdom. It's better than lacking them. But there are geniuses like von Doom who have high IQs, but who use their brains for evil.

And even smart people can make dumb decisions.

Many geniuses ignore God. How smart is *that*? "[The wise men] have rejected the word of the LORD; so what wisdom do they have?" (Jeremiah 8:9 NKJV). Don't trust in your brain. Depend on God.

INVISIBLE WOMAN
26.
Amazing Invisible Power

Susan Storm is famous for bending light waves to make herself disappear. She just vanishes! That's why she's called Invisible Woman. But her greatest power is how she controls large masses of unseen energy. She can create force fields to protect herself from bullets, and she can knock people down with energy. She may not look like it, but she's the most powerful member of the Fantastic Four.

The comicbooks say she does these things by drawing power from hyperspace. Now, many unseen energies and power fields *do* exist, and God created them. "For by Him all things were created. . .visible and invisible" (Colossians 1:16 NKJV).

God has given angels astonishing powers, and they use invisible energy to do miracles. One time, Herod Agrippa threw Peter in prison. At night, Peter was sleeping, bound with chains between two soldiers. Then an angel woke Peter up. Immediately his chains snapped and fell off. The angel told him to follow, so

Peter did. They passed two guard posts and came to the outer iron gate—and it opened (Acts 12:5–10).

The angel never touched the chains or the gate. He just snapped the chains with invisible power and opened the iron gate with a thrust of energy. Many Christians believe that when their physical bodies are resurrected, they too will have such powers (see Psalm 8:4–5; Matthew 22:30; 1 Corinthians 15:42–44). Your physical body will be changed when Jesus returns to Earth. And it will receive great power.

Sue never showed off her powers. She was a strong, quiet person. Reed was the leader of the group, but it was Sue's motherly influence that kept the Fantastic Four together. Many believers are like Sue, shy and quiet, but they're often the ones who move mountains through prayer. They pray a spiritual "force field" around their homes and families (Job 1:10). Attacks bounced off Sue's force fields, and God can shield you too. "The LORD is my strength and my shield" (Psalm 28:7 NKJV).

Don't worry if you seem weaker than other people. Think about it: How are you truly strong anyway? "'Not by might nor by power, but by My Spirit,' says the LORD" (Zechariah 4:6 NKJV). Even when you feel weak, you can still be strong. Paul said, "Be strong in the Lord and in the power of His might" (Ephesians 6:10 NKJV).

Attention: Before you ask your parents to let you watch the *Fantastic Four* movies, make sure you read the devotion "Beauty Is Skin Deep" first.

THE TORCH

27.
Hot Heads and Pride

Johnny Storm can cause his body to burst into flames, hot enough to melt metal, and fly through the air at high speed. That's why he's called Torch. He can also hurl fireballs at his enemies. If he really concentrates, he can go into "supernova" mode and burn as hot as the sun.

Can people actually survive great heat? If God does a miracle, yes. When Shadrach, Meshach, and Abednego refused to worship Nebuchadnezzar's idol, he ordered his guards to toss them into a blazing furnace. They fell into the flames then got up and walked around. The fire didn't harm them. Not a hair on their heads was singed, and their clothing didn't light on fire (Daniel 3:8–27).

One time, an angel *flew* in the midst of flames, like the Torch. "As Manoah and his wife watched, the LORD did an amazing thing. As the flames from the altar shot up toward the sky, the angel of the LORD ascended in the fire" (Judges 13:19–20 NLT). And Elijah called down fire from heaven three times (1 Kings 18:36–39; 2 Kings 1:9–12).

Johnny Storm was hotheaded and rash. (A rash person is someone who acts without thinking.) Reed told him, "You need to. . .think before you act."[46] But that wasn't Johnny's style. When a heat-seeking missile was flying toward them, he decided to leap off the building, change into the Torch, and lead the missile away. His sister Sue ordered, "Don't even *think* about it!" Johnny joked, "Never do," and leaped.[47]

He was convinced that he was "hot" in other ways too, and he constantly used his good looks and powers to impress women.

He only had one crash-and-burn—and that was after chasing the Silver Surfer. But in real life, people who are rash and prideful have many accidents. The Bible warns, "Pride goes before destruction, and a haughty spirit before a fall" (Proverbs 16:18 NKJV).

You might know somebody who's a lot like Johnny, but this message is for you also. You may have talent or good looks and think you're pretty hot stuff. Watch out! God will make sure you're humbled. It happened to King Uzziah. "He was marvelously helped until he was strong. But when he became strong, his heart was so proud that he acted corruptly" (2 Chronicles 26:15–16 NASB). And God brought him down.

Despite Johnny's flaws, he was bold, self-sacrificial,

and honest. God can make a hero out of anyone. So don't give up on yourself. Ask God to keep you humble and to help you think before you act. You'll avoid burnout.

THE THING

28.
Unhappy With Your Looks

When the Fantastic Four were caught in a cosmic storm, Ben Grimm changed the most. Afterward, he weighed five hundred pounds, and his whole body looked like it was made of orange rocks. One newsperson said he looked like some kind of monster or thing. That's where he got his name, the Thing. Ben often complained about his looks, and he asked Reed to find a way to make him look human again.

Although he knew that the cosmic storm had caused his condition, Ben still blamed God. He said, "If there's a God, He hates me."[48] The truth was, Ben *did* believe in God. He was just constantly complaining, like the Jewish father Tevye in *Fiddler on the Roof*. In fact, like Tevye, Ben was Jewish. This came out in a comic titled "Remembrance of Things Past." Benjamin Grimm is, after all, a Jewish name.

When Ben returned to the neighborhood where he'd grown up, he battled the villain Powderkeg. In the fight, Powderkeg wounded an old Jewish man, Mr.

Sheckerberg. Ben thought Sheckerberg was going to die, so he prayed a Hebrew prayer, the *Sh'ma Yisrael*, often prayed over the dying. When Sheckerberg survived, he asked Ben why he never talked about his faith. Ben said he didn't want people to think all Jews were monsters like him.[49]

It always came back to Ben's obsession with his looks. Many people are unhappy about their appearance and ask God why He made them that way. But Paul asked a different question: "Will the thing formed say to him who formed it, 'Why have you made me like this?'" (Romans 9:20 NKJV). And it *was* Ben's rocky body that gave him great strength.

Some Bible superheroes also had image issues: "Some brave and experienced warriors from the tribe of Gad. . .were expert with both shield and spear, as fierce as lions. . . . The weakest among them could take on a hundred regular troops, and the strongest could take on a thousand!" (1 Chronicles 12:8, 14 NLT). They were so powerful, they were unstoppable. The New Living Translation says they were "as fierce as lions," but the New King James Version gives a more accurate translation. It says their "faces were like the faces of lions." They weren't good-looking, but they had great power, which they used for good.

Johnny Storm asked, "He *does* have some kind of rock-like heart, doesn't he?"[50] Indeed Ben did. Despite his looks and constant grumbling, Ben was courageous, selfless, and loyal. And inner qualities are, after all, what counts. "Man looks at the outward appearance, but the LORD looks at the heart" (1 Samuel 16:7 NASB).

SILVER SURFER
29.
A TENDER CONSCIENCE

Silver Surfer was one of the most powerful foes the Fantastic Four ever fought—and his master, Galactus, had the power to destroy planets. He lived by devouring the energy of entire worlds. One day, Galactus was about to destroy an alien world when Norrin Radd, who lived there, offered to lead him to other planets. So Galactus gave Radd power and covered him with silver material that protected him in outer space. Then he gave him a silver surfboard to travel on.

One day, Silver Surfer arrived at Earth. He saw how many living things would be destroyed and wanted to spare it, but Galactus was so hungry he refused to wait. So Silver Surfer rebelled against Galactus, and he left.

The Surfer sometimes used his power selfishly. But his conscience always bothered him. In *Silver Surfer* comic issue 1, he needed money, so he broke into a bank. Then he realized what he was doing and repented.[51] In *Silver Surfer* issue 3, he saved a woman's life, only to have police think he was an enemy and shoot at him. He vowed revenge. Before attacking, he spread out his arms, looked up, and cried out, "Forgive me for what I am about to do!"[52] To whom was he praying? God. Even though he wanted revenge, his conscience was already bothering him.

King David was also a man of great power with a tender heart. Although sometimes he was moved to act by anger, lust, or a longing for power, he always repented. David loved God, and though he sinned, he sincerely repented (Psalm 51).

David had created a massive empire that stretched from Egypt to the Euphrates River. It was so huge that David wondered if his army was strong enough to hold it together. He failed to keep trusting God and decided to count how many soldiers he had. This angered God. He sent an angel to kill the Israelites David was counting on.

When David saw the angel, he prayed, "Was it not I who ordered the fighting men to be counted? I, the shepherd, have sinned and done wrong. These are but sheep. What have they done? LORD my God, let your hand fall on me. . .but do not let this plague remain on your people" (1 Chronicles 21:17 NIV). So God stopped.

How do you act when you're given power? Do you use it to take what you want? God warns that He will judge the powerful if they mistreat the weak. So have a tender conscience.

DAREDEVIL
30.
See Things Differently

Matt Murdock was just a boy in New York City when he was accidentally blinded by a radioactive chemical. It robbed him of his sight but greatly increased his hearing. He could now "see" by sound vibrations, like bats can "see" with echolocation. Then, after his father was murdered, Matt decided to become a crime fighter. He learned several martial arts and began his career as Daredevil. A daredevil is "a reckless person who enjoys doing dangerous things."

Daredevil was known as "the man without fear." He had to be. Remember, he had no superpowers. Anyone can learn martial arts, but some people naturally have quick reflexes and great strength. These qualities, together with courage, transform them into champions.

Three thousand years ago, another mighty warrior was a daredevil and a man without fear. His name was Benaiah, and he belonged to an elite group of warriors called David's Mighty Men (2 Samuel 23:8, 20). One day, Benaiah leaped down into a pit during a snow-storm and killed a lion. Why Benaiah jumped into a small space with a wild lion, we have no idea. But after a fierce fight, the beast was dead.

Then there was an Egyptian giant, "a spectacu-lar man" (2 Samuel 23:21 NKJV). All Benaiah had was a staff, and the giant came at him with a spear. Most men would have run. But Benaiah snatched Spectacular Man's spear from him and slew him with it.

Marvel's blind superhero illustrates another import-ant lesson. Paul said, "We walk by faith, not by sight" (2 Corinthians 5:7 KJV). God will often ask you to trust that He will do a miracle, and He wants you to step out in faith. When ten lepers begged Jesus to heal them, He told them to show themselves to the priests—as if they were already healed. They obeyed, and "as they went, they were cleansed" (Luke 17:14 NKJV).

God probably won't ask you to leap down into a snowy pit to battle a lion, nor will He ask you to fight supervillains blindfolded. But He may ask you to do things that require great faith, just as He did for Abra-ham. The Bible says, "By faith Abraham obeyed when he was called to go. . . . And he went out, not knowing where he was going" (Hebrews 11:8 NKJV).

God will lead you even when you can't see the path

ahead. He promises, "I will bring the blind by a way they did not know; I will lead them in paths they have not known" (Isaiah 42:16 NKJV). "The LORD is the one who goes ahead of you; He will be with you. He will not fail you or forsake you" (Deuteronomy 31:8 NASB).

DR. STRANGE
31.
The Great Power of God

Stephen Strange was a surgeon whose career came to an end when he broke the bones in his hands. In the movie *Dr. Strange*, he then traveled to Nepal where he met a five-hundred-year-old sorcerer named the Ancient One. Dr. Strange learned from her and was soon fighting evil sorcerers like Mordo with magic spells.

Is this sorcery of God? Some people argue that magical power is neither good nor evil, and they say that many superheroes draw on unseen energy to fly, teleport, and shoot energy. What's the difference between Dr. Strange stopping a sorcerer's power bolt with a shield of magical force, and Invisible Woman stopping an energy beam with a force field? Isn't "magic" simply a different kind of energy?

Perhaps, except that in Dr. Strange's world, this power comes from spiritual beings. In the comicbooks, Dr. Strange calls on the Vishanti—either Hoggoth, Agamotto, or Oshtur. When reciting magic spells, he usually calls on these three beings for power.

Hoggoth is called "the Lord of Hosts." (The Bible also describes God as the "Lord of Hosts" over 250 times.) Agamotto is known as "the Light of Truth." (Jesus said, "I am the light," and "I am. . .the truth" [John 8:12; 14:6 NKJV.]) It all sounds good so far.

But then things take a strange turn. Oshtur is called "Lady of the Skies." It so happens that Ishtar, an ancient goddess, was called Ashteroth by the Hebrews. The similarity between the names Oshtur, Ishtar, and Ashteroth is deliberate. The writer had wicked Ishtar in mind. What's more, one of Ishtar's titles is Queen of Heaven.

In the days of the early Christians, "a man named Simon had been a sorcerer there for many years, amazing the people of Samaria and claiming to be someone great. Everyone. . .spoke of him as 'the Great One—the Power of God.' They listened closely to him because for a long time he had astounded them with his magic" (Acts 8:9–11 NLT).

Simon practiced dark magic, but because the Samaritans believed in God, he talked about his sorcery in godly terms and claimed his power came from heaven. This allowed him to claim the title "the Power of God." Yet Simon's power came from evil spirits, and he was "full of bitter envy and. . .a prisoner of sin" (Acts 8:23

GNT). When Philip came to Samaria preaching Jesus and performing miracles, Simon realized that God's power was greater than his sorcery.

Don't be misled. *Dr. Strange* is a fascinating film with many amazing special effects, but it does little to reveal the truth about the astonishing God we serve.

WOLVERINE

32.
Undoing Past Mistakes

In the movie *X-Men: Days of Future Past*, Charles Xavier, Magneto, and a few others were the last mutants in a very dark future. All others had been slain by robots called Sentinels. How did this happen? Well, Mystique had killed Dr. Trask, the creator of the Sentinels, but she was soon captured, and her DNA was used to make the Sentinels deadlier. Mystique could change to be like anyone else, and now the Sentinels could match the powers of every mutant.

However, a mutant named Kitty Pryde could send people's minds into the past, so Xavier had her send Wolverine into the past to stop Mystique from killing Trask. Together with other mutants, Wolverine stopped Mystique. Then because she, a mutant, saved the president, he decided *not* to authorize the Sentinel program. So it never happened. Wolverine returned to a very different future where all the mutants were alive and happy.

If only life *were* that easy!

Have you ever messed up so badly that you wished you could go back and do it again? Probably you have . . .more than once. This is especially true if your past causes you a lot of pain.

You can't go back in time and do things over. But here's the good news: despite everything bad that happened, God's Spirit *can* "make all things new" (Revelation 21:5 NKJV). His forgiveness can undo the pain of the past. It doesn't matter how greatly you've sinned. "If we confess our sins, he. . .will forgive us our sins and purify us from *all* unrighteousness" (1 John 1:9 NIV, emphasis added). God also said, "Though your sins are like scarlet, they shall be as white as snow; though they are red as crimson, they shall be like wool" (Isaiah 1:18 NIV).

There was a man in Jesus' day who was possessed by thousands of demons. His name was Legion. (A legion was 5,120 men.) This man was a supervillain with astonishing strength. He could snap iron chains, so he couldn't be bound. And he was tormented! He lived in the tombs with dead bodies and cried out night and day, cutting himself with stones (Mark 5:2–5). You *wouldn't* want to meet this guy in a dark alley.

Yet after Jesus cast the demons out of him, he ended up peacefully sitting and talking with Jesus (Mark 5:15). He had a brand-new life! Jesus can transform the darkest, most hopeless people. He's done it for others and can do it for you. When God forgives your sins, it's as if you had never sinned.

ADAM WARLOCK
33.
Don't Accept a Fake

You might wonder, "What would it be like if someone made comics showing what Jesus would be like as a superhero?" Well, Marvel Comics did that. Editor Roy Thomas didn't believe that Jesus was God, or even the Son of God, but he created a superhero based on Jesus' life.

There was a Marvel character called "Him," a perfect human who had been created by scientists. Thomas had "Him" leave Earth and meet a man named Herbert Wyndham. This genius had made a paradise world and placed men on it who were free from evil. But there was a problem: Wyndham had morphed a wolf into a super-being. This evil monster then went to Wyndham's planet, ruled it as a dictator, and turned the humans violent.

Wyndham gave "Him" the name Adam Warlock then sent him to defeat the wolf. Warlock did stop it, but then he fell in love with himself and thought he was God. So people rejected Warlock and crucified him. But he raised himself from the dead, and a new religion began, worshipping him as God.

Well, now. This *started out* as a good parable. Adam Warlock is like Jesus. God sent His Son to the world just like Wyndham sent Warlock. The evil wolf-being represents the devil. The people he corrupted are like Earth's humans. And the religion that worshipped Warlock is like Christianity. But, because Thomas didn't believe that Jesus was God—one with His Father— Thomas's story ended all wrong.

Jesus didn't dream up the idea that He was God. Jesus truly *was* God, and was since before time began. The Bible says, "In the beginning was the Word [Jesus], and the Word was with God, and the Word was God" (John 1:1 NIV). John later said, "No one has ever seen God, but the one and only Son, who is himself God. . . has made him known" (John 1:18 NIV).

Thomas called his superhero Warlock. Bad news: a warlock is a male witch or sorcerer. Some people in Jesus' day, who hated Jesus, *also* said He was an evil sorcerer.

Be very careful. Just because someone talks about Jesus doesn't mean that what they're saying about Him is right. They could have strange ideas. The apostle Paul warned, "Actually, there is no 'other gospel,' but I say this because there are some people who are upsetting you and trying to change the gospel of Christ" (Galatians 1:7 GNT).

Don't be misled by people's imaginations. Don't accept a fake Savior. Don't let anyone hand you a cheap substitute. The world is full of deceivers—so beware!

IRON MAN
34.
When You're Stressed

In the end of the movie *The Avengers*, Tony Stark guided a nuclear missile through a hole in space where it exploded, wiping out enemy aliens. It nearly killed him too. That was scary enough. But then his Iron Man suit ran out of power, and Stark fell to Earth. He was certain he would die. But at the last second, Hulk caught him.

That was an exciting ending, but imagine you were Tony Stark! It wouldn't have just been exciting. It would have been terrifying. It would have left you shaken up. And that's what happened. Iron Man is powerful, but under the armor Tony Stark is only human, and humans suffer if they go through strong feelings of fear.

The movie *Iron Man 3* picked up the story after this, and it showed Stark suffering from fear and stress. He complained, "I build neat stuff, got a great girl, occasionally save the world. So why can't I sleep?"[53] For months, he kept himself busy making Iron Man suits. This helped him not think about his frightening experience.

Even worry, if it goes on for a long time, can make you sick. You've heard people say, "He's under a lot of stress." They might be talking about someone who has a difficult test. Or they might be talking about someone who has to walk past a bully's house every day to get to school.

Paul had problems and stress too. He wrote, "We are hard-pressed on every side, yet not crushed" (2 Corinthians 4:8 NKJV). But when things got worse, he said, "We were crushed and overwhelmed beyond our ability to endure, and we thought we would never live through it" (2 Corinthians 1:8 NLT).

David said to God, "I cry to you for help when my heart is overwhelmed" (Psalm 61:2 NLT). Once, when he and his warriors were away, raiders attacked their homes and took their wives and children. When David's men returned, their town was burned and their families gone. They wept until they had no more tears. His men gave up, but "David strengthened himself in the LORD" (1 Samuel 30:6 NKJV). God told David and his men to chase the raiders, so they did. They found them, fought them, and got their families back—*all* of them (1 Samuel 30:3–19).

Sometimes you'll feel overwhelmed. When you do, you may want to give up. Instead, be like David: remind yourself that God loves you and can do the impossible. Then you'll be encouraged to pray. And when you pray, refuse to give up.

GAMBIT
35.
Winners and Losers

Gambit is a mutant with the power to charge up energy inside things. Then he throws the object, and when it strikes its target, it explodes. Gambit likes to throw playing cards, partly because he always has some handy, and partly because they're so small he can charge them quickly. Besides, even one card explodes like a grenade.

Gambit's name has an unusual meaning. A gambit is an opening move in chess where a player is willing to lose some pawns in order to win in the end. So a gambit is a bold gamble. Gambit loves gambling and is willing to take huge risks. His real name, by the way, is Remy LeBeau. *Le Beau* is French for "the handsome one."

But there's more to Gambit than good looks. He once said, "The only difference between a winner and a loser is character."[54] (Character is good habits, like honesty, that make you strong.) Gambit was right. In card games, you have good fortune *and* misfortune. In life, misfortunes include poor health or losing money.

Some people give up during hard times. Those with strong character refuse to surrender. So your character decides whether you win or lose.

You can lose it all, like Job did in the Bible, but if you have good character and continue trusting God, you'll still be blessed. Many people turn their backs on God when it seems He's turned His back on them. That's one choice. The other is to stay faithful, even when you're suffering and life seems terrible. Remember, after Job had suffered, God blessed him even more.

Paul said that "suffering produces perseverance" (Romans 5:3 NIV). To persevere means to patiently keep going. Patience and perseverance will help you overcome. "Take the prophets. . .as an example of suffering and patience. Indeed we count them blessed who endure. You have heard of the perseverance of Job and seen the end intended by the Lord—that the Lord is very compassionate and merciful" (James 5:10–11 NKJV).

Gambit said, "If I learnt anything about life, it's this: always play the hand you're dealt."[55] In card games, you often get a poor hand. But you can't just throw your cards on the table and demand new ones. Yet people often complain about the things God lets happen. And they insist that He immediately fix all their problems. You have to learn to make the best of your situation, even if you think you have a losing hand.

As Gambit said, "the only difference between a winner and a loser is character." Do *you* have character?

BLACK PANTHER
36.
Ready to Do Battle

The Black Panther is the name of a powerful superhero. His actual name is T'Challa, and he's leader of the small African nation of Wakanda. Like the black leopard he's named after, Black Panther has super-sharp senses and great strength, speed, and fighting abilities. He first appeared in *Captain America: Civil War*, where he matched Captain America blow for blow.

Black Panther wears a costume made from vibranium, a super-hard metal. Even bullets can't pierce it. He also has claws made of vibranium. Where did this amazing metal come from? Long ago, a meteorite struck Wakanda, leaving a lot of the metal there. It also gave off radiation, which entered the nearby plants. This made a mysterious heart-shaped herb give special powers to whoever ate it. Only the Black Panther, king of Wakanda, is allowed to eat this plant, so only he has superpowers.

In the movie *Captain America: Civil War*, the old King T'Chaka was killed by a terrorist bomb while speaking at the United Nations. Immediately, the king's son T'Challa ran after the terrorist. Even though T'Challa was now king, he plunged into battle like a regular warrior.

David in the Bible was also a warrior. Even though he was king of Israel, he often led armies into battle. In one battle before he became ruler, David led a small patrol through some fields, and they ran into a company of Philistines. A company is one hundred men. David's men panicked when the Philistines charged. They fled, and only David and a warrior named Eleazar stayed to fight. When the battle ended, only David and Eleazar were standing. The entire company of Philistines was dead (2 Samuel 23:9–10; 1 Chronicles 11:12–14).

Even when he was old, King David often left his throne to plunge into battle. Once he was fighting when Ishbi-Benob, a fierce Philistine giant, rushed up and tried to kill him. Fortunately, David's bodyguard rescued him. Then David's men told him, "Never again will you go out with us to battle" (2 Samuel 21:17 NIV). They had to hold the king *back* from fighting.

You may not be the ruler of a fabulously rich African nation or the king of Israel, and you probably don't have superpowers, but you too can step up in times of need. Being a superhero may seem cool, but they're often just street fighters in fancy costumes. David and T'Challa weren't afraid to leave their thrones, throw off their royal robes, and fight for a worthy cause. Are you willing to do what needs to be done?

STAR-LORD
37.
Respect God's Power

The movie *Guardians of the Galaxy* tried hard to be funny, and it is sometimes downright silly. But it deals with a very serious subject—a plot to destroy the planet Xandar, capital of the Nova Empire.

When Peter Quill (Star-Lord) was a child, aliens took him from Earth. He became a space pirate, and one day he stole a mysterious Orb from a temple. Later he asked, "This Orb has a real shiny. . .Ark of the Covenant. . .sort of vibe. What is it?"[56] It turns out the Orb was only the outer shell. Inside was a Power Stone, a very powerful Infinity Gem.

This story has a complicated plot, but the basic idea is that the alien Ronan wanted to destroy Xandar. The Power Stone could do that, but few beings could handle it without being destroyed. Thanos could, so Ronan was desperate to take him the Stone.

A team of unusual friends joined Quill. They were Gamora, Rocket Raccoon, Groot, and Drax. They became the Guardians of the Galaxy. In the end, Ronan seized the Power Stone and was about to destroy Xandar when Quill snatched it from him. All the Guardians joined hands with him, so its power didn't kill Quill—and Xandar was spared.

Humans often have no idea of how terrific God's power is. Once, the Israelites wanted to defeat the Philistines, so they brought the ark of the covenant to the battlefield. This was a gold-covered chest, and the glory of God sometimes appeared as a bright cloud over it.

The Israelites, however, treated the ark like a good luck charm—so God let the Philistines capture it. They took it to Ashdod and set it before their idol. They thought Dagon had defeated Israel's God. But Dagon's idol fell down before the ark. Then a terrible sickness swept the city. Terrified, the Philistines sent it to Gath, but plague broke out there also.

The Philistines finally respected God's power and returned the ark to Israel. But many Israelites didn't have much respect for God either. Seventy of them became curious and peeked inside the ark—and died (1 Samuel 6:19).

God is holy and all-powerful, but many people are only curious about Him. They just give a quick peek to see if there's anything to this "God" thing—and they usually learn nothing. Others have no respect for God. They believe science is wiser and more powerful than the Lord. But remember: God created the entire universe. He's far greater and more powerful than even an Infinity Gem.

DEADPOOL
38.
Super But No Hero

Wade Wilson (Deadpool) was a supervillain and downright evil when he appeared in the movie *X-Men Origins: Wolverine*. But then the producers gave Deadpool his own movie and tried to make him someone viewers could identify with.

Is he a hero? When a friend called Deadpool a superhero, he admitted, "I may be super, but I'm no hero."[57] If he's not a superhero or a supervillain, what *is* he? He's a foul-mouthed person with superpowers who enjoys killing people. Be warned: this movie is rated R (Restricted) for a reason. Don't even *think* of asking your parents to let you see it.

In the movie, Wade had cancer throughout his body. Then some scientists promised, "We can give you abilities most men can only dream of."[58] But though Wade received great power, his face and mind were nearly destroyed. He also had a new name: Deadpool.

Deadpool used nonstop dirty language and told filthy jokes. Sailors were famous for swearing, so

Captain America asked, "What's the deal with all that potty-mouth stuff, huh? Why does every movie these days have to feel like a sailor wrote the script?"[59] It sounds like he was talking about the movie *Deadpool*.

The Bible says, "Obscene stories, foolish talk, and coarse jokes—these are not for you" (Ephesians 5:4 NLT). So this movie is not for you either.

Many people think it's funny the way Deadpool guns people down in the streets, taking a sick delight in killing. And right after the noble Colossus talks about being a superhero and the greatness of showing mercy to your enemies, Deadpool shoots a man in the head. Right in front of Colossus. Clearly, Deadpool thinks all superhero virtues are a joke.

Deadpool is very much like King Saul in the Bible, a strong warrior who later became mentally sick. Saul had been a powerful fighter and had saved Israel many times from her enemies (1 Samuel 14:47–48). But after he kept disobeying God, the Lord took His Spirit from Saul, leaving him open to the devil's attacks. "The Spirit of the LORD had left Saul, and the LORD sent a tormenting spirit that filled him with depression and fear" (1 Samuel 16:14 NLT).

And no surprise, Saul—like Deadpool—had a dirty mouth (1 Samuel 20:30 NLT).

Why was *Deadpool* so successful that the producers made a second movie? The reason is simple: many people today identify with Deadpool's selfishness and potty humor. But he has a sick outlook on life. . .and it's nothing to laugh about.

ELEKTRA
39.
Don't Seek Revenge

Elektra was the daughter of a rich Greek businessman, Nikolas Natchios. Elektra was a young woman with fantastic fighting skills. One day, she met a blind lawyer, Matt Murdock, and they fell in love. She couldn't possibly have guessed that he was the superhero Daredevil.

When a criminal named Kingpin sent the assassin Bullseye to kill Elektra's father, Daredevil tried to stop him, but Bullseye managed to kill her father anyway. Elektra didn't know what had happened. She thought Daredevil had done it, so she vowed revenge on him. She later wounded Daredevil, removed his mask, and was shocked to see that it was Matt Murdock under the mask. Too late she learned that Daredevil hadn't killed her father.

This is one reason why the Bible forbids revenge. You often don't have all the facts and can easily misjudge. Also, your brand of "justice" might be very harsh. Matt Murdock once told a priest, "Justice isn't a sin, Father." The priest replied, "No, but vengeance is."[60] You will sometimes be tempted to make others hurt like you've been hurt. But God warns, "Do not say, 'I'll do to them as they have done to me; I'll pay them back for what they did'" (Proverbs 24:29 NIV).

In the Bible, Abner, general of Israel's army, was fleeing after a battle, and a warrior named Asahel chased him. The warrior was the brother of Joab, Judah's top general. Abner tried to persuade Asahel not to come after him, but Asahel wouldn't go away. So just as Asahel was about to catch him, Abner killed Asahel with his spear.

Joab didn't care that Abner had tried to spare Asahel. All he could think of was that Abner had killed his brother, and he was determined to get revenge. Sometime later, when Abner visited David to make peace, Joab took Abner aside. He pretended he wanted to speak with him. Instead, he murdered him (2 Samuel 3:12–39). Joab felt right about what he'd done, but David wept over Abner's death. He was upset at how Joab had hated him and plotted to kill him.

Seeking revenge usually starts with holding a grudge against someone and refusing to forgive that person. The more you think about the wrong done to you or the way you were offended, the madder you get. And the madder you get, the more you want to hurt the other person. The Bible tells you to chase after love, not revenge. Love keeps no record of wrongs. The Lord said, "Do not seek revenge or bear a grudge against anyone. . .but love your neighbor as yourself" (Leviticus 19:18 NIV).

SPIDER-MAN
40.
Prayers and Complaints

In the comicbooks, Peter Parker (Spider-Man) was warned that a deadly foe would attack him because he'd been bitten by a radioactive spider. Since his relationship to spiders put him in danger, Peter prayed, "Hey, God? It's Peter again. Listen, not that I'm complaining or anything, but next incarnation. . .you think you could have me get bitten by a radioactive Jennifer Lopez?"[61] (Lopez was a beautiful actress. Peter was joking, of course.)

When he said "next incarnation," Peter was talking about reincarnation. But even though people have some false ideas, don't give up on them. Meet them where they're at, like Jesus did with the Samaritan woman. He said, "You Samaritans know very little about the one you worship" (John 4:22 NLT). Then He told her that God accepted anyone who worshipped Him "in spirit and in truth" (verse 24).

Paul told the Greeks, "As I was walking along I saw your many shrines. And one of your altars had this inscription on it: 'To an Unknown God.' This God, whom you worship without knowing, is the one I'm telling you about" (Acts 17:23 NLT).

Peter Parker often complained to the "Unknown God." But he also prayed prayers of gratitude. He and Mary Jane Watson were married, and Peter prayed, "God. . .I know I complain a lot, and I know that you and me, we've got issues, but right now, just for tonight. . . Thank you for her. Thank you."[62]

The Bible says, "I will bless the LORD at all times: his praise shall continually be in my mouth" (Psalm 34:1 KJV). Yes, you are to bless the Lord "at *all* times," even when things go wrong. That's difficult for many people. It's easy to feel grateful when you have no big problems. But see what happens when things go wrong. Even Job, after months of suffering (Job 7:3) filled many chapters with his complaints to God (Job 23:2–4).

The Bible says, "Anyone who comes to him must believe that he exists and that he rewards those who earnestly seek him" (Hebrews 11:6 NIV). Peter Parker was often in the first group. He believed God existed, but he didn't think He was usually willing to answer his prayers. So Peter complained.

The second group not only believes that God exists, but also trusts that He will one day answer their prayers. If you believe that, you can have a positive attitude. Even if you don't think He will give you all your rewards in *this* life, if you believe He will bless you in heaven, you can endure hard times now.

PROFESSOR X

41.
Beware What You Think

Mutants like Charles Xavier are able to read other people's thoughts. You may wonder, "Are such abilities real outside of movies?" Yes, they certainly are. For example, God knows all the time what every single person on Earth is thinking. David told Solomon that "the LORD sees every heart and knows every plan and thought" (1 Chronicles 28:9 NLT).

Jesus had the ability to read minds too. He once told a sick man, "Your sins are forgiven." Some religious teachers thought, "Why does this fellow talk like that? He's blaspheming! Who can forgive sins but God alone?" Jesus *knew* what they were thinking, so He asked, "Why are you thinking these things?" (Mark 2:5–8 NIV). Jesus could even see into the minds of those some distance away (John 1:47–48).

The Holy Spirit also gave Jesus supernatural knowledge about people far off. Once He saw His disciples in trouble even though they were four miles away in the dark. "That night, the boat was in the middle of the lake, and he was alone on land. He saw the disciples straining at the oars, because the wind was against them" (Mark 6:47–48 NIV).

Charles Xavier frequently sent his own thoughts into another person's mind. God does this too. He rarely talks out loud, but usually speaks in a gentle, quiet voice, planting a thought in your mind that you should or shouldn't do something. Many times, however, what you think is God's voice is just your own thoughts (Jeremiah 23:21, 26), so be careful. You *might* be hearing from God, or you might *not* be.

When Magneto was about to kidnap Rogue in the movie *X-Men*, Xavier took over one of Magneto's men and spoke through his mouth to Magneto. God, however, doesn't usually control people's minds against their will. He doesn't usually cause people to do or say something they normally wouldn't.

Many people have the idea that thoughts aren't important. They believe that if what they think doesn't hurt anyone, then it's their own business, nothing for God to be concerned about. But thoughts are real. They aren't simply unimportant shadows. They're the powerful generals that command your entire body.

God not only knows your thoughts, but He will also one day judge you for your actions—whether you failed to act on good thoughts, or acted on selfish ones. But remember: a passing bad thought won't ruin you if you don't act on it.

Be careful what you think. As David prayed, "May my words and my thoughts be acceptable to you, O Lord" (Psalm 19:14 GNT).

MAGNETO

42.

WRONG IDEAS ABOUT GOD

In the first *X-Men* movie, Senator Robert Kelly constantly warned that mutants were dangerous. So Magneto kidnapped him to change *him* into a mutant. He asked, "Are you a *God-fearing* man, Senator?" Then Magneto thought about the question he'd just asked, and said, "That is such a strange phrase. I've always thought of God as a teacher; a bringer of light, wisdom, and understanding."[63] Magneto decided it was wrong to fear God.

Since "God is love" and "there is no fear in love" (1 John 4:8, 18 KJV), many people think that He can't be the God of the Old Testament who judged people. They think a loving God wouldn't punish anyone.

As Magneto went to turn on the mutation machine, the terrified Senator asked what he was doing. Magneto answered, "Let's just say, God works too slow."[64] Because God wasn't acting to stop his enemies, Magneto decided to stop them himself.

Magneto would have agreed with the Jews who

said, "The LORD will not do good, neither will he do evil" (Zephaniah 1:12 KJV). Not only does God not act *immediately* when people think their enemies need to be judged, but often He seems not to act at *all*. For example, many people ask, "Why doesn't God stop terrorists from killing people?"

The answer is that God *does* stop them—and He uses America and other nations to do it. God hears the prayers of millions of people and has caused many nations to fight and defeat terrorists. Time and again in the Bible, when the Israelites were beaten down by enemies, God inspired warriors to rise up, do battle, and defeat them.

Seeing how God often uses men to stop other men from doing evil, many people get the idea that God isn't doing anything. They think they must take matters into their own hands to get justice. Often God *does* call you to fight for your rights, but there are also times when you're powerless. When that happens, God promises, "It is mine to avenge; I will repay" (Deuteronomy 32:35 NIV).

In the movie *X-Men United*, Magneto's belief that God was far away drove him to try to murder billions of people. Magneto dared to do such a horrible thing because he didn't fear God. He believed that God wouldn't do anything to him in this life—and wouldn't judge him in the next life either.

It's wise to fear God. Fearing God is not negative. "The fear of the LORD is pure" (Psalm 19:9 NIV). If you fear God because you know He judges people after they die, you'll be motivated to do good.

THE AVENGERS
43.
Watch What You Say

Nick Fury explained his reason for creating the Avengers: "The idea was to bring together a group of remarkable people to see if they. . .could work together . . .to fight the battles that we never could."[65] It sounds so easy: because they were the good guys, they'd easily come together to work as a team and fight supervillains that normal people couldn't.

Now, it's true that a team of superheroes *is* stronger than each superhero on his own. The Bible says, "Two people are better off than one, for they can help each other succeed. If one person falls, the other can reach out and help. . . . A person standing alone can be attacked and defeated, but two can stand back-to-back and conquer" (Ecclesiastes 4:9–10, 12 NLT).

But Bruce Banner (the Hulk) doubted they could work together. He asked, "What are we, a team? No, no, no. We're a chemical mixture that makes chaos."[66] He meant that they were powerful chemicals that didn't belong together—that would just cause an explosion if they were mixed. But Captain America had hope. When Tony Stark asked how they could defeat Ultron, Cap answered, "Together."[67]

But Iron Man and Captain America criticized each other from the beginning. Iron Man constantly took jabs at Cap's old-fashioned ways. Cap in turn constantly criticized Iron Man's pride. It came as no surprise when, in the movie *Captain America: Civil War*, they openly battled each other. When you work with others in a team, you have to be humble and watch what you say to make things work. You'll need to because many people have large egos and short tempers.

Civil war also broke out in ancient Israel over proud people arguing. David's son Absalom had rebelled but was defeated. With Absalom gone, Israel (the northern tribes) spoke of bringing the king back to Jerusalem. But the men of Judah beat them to it. Shortly after they'd ferried King David across the Jordan River, the Israelites showed up, asking why Judah hadn't let them help. They began arguing, but "the words of the men of Judah were fiercer than the words of the men of Israel" (2 Samuel 19:43 NKJV).

The men of Judah won the argument by yelling more angrily and fiercely than the Israelites, but their "victory" came with a big price tag. All the men from the northern tribes left David—and the civil war was on. . .*again*.

Beware of pride and rivalry. They can grow until they destroy unity and wreck the good that a team could do.

WOLVERINE

44.
Immortal Warriors

Some superheroes have been around so long that fans wonder why they never grow old. And it's not just that time goes slower in comicbooks than the real world. These superheroes are *really* old! The opening scene of *X-Men Origins: Wolverine* says that Wolverine was born in the 1830s. That means he is about 180 years old. And he's still going strong. Black Widow (Natasha) was born during the 1930s yet still has the beauty of a young woman.

How do they do it? Well, while Natasha was training as a spy, she was scientifically changed, which gives her very long life and youth. The comics never explain how. But there *is* an explanation for Wolverine: his body has the power to heal super quickly. This also slows down his aging, letting him live a long time.

But is such long life possible? That brings up another question: Did ancient people actually live hundreds of years? For example, the Bible says Methuselah lived to be 969 years old (Genesis 5:27).

Recently, scientists have learned that aging is mostly caused by damage to people's DNA. It adds up over the years. Scientists are exploring how to repair cells to make people live longer. They think they'll be able to make humans live for hundreds of years. Suddenly the idea of patriarchs living 969 years doesn't seem so strange. Even Wolverine seems young at 180 years old.

Here's something you probably didn't know: *Turritopsis dohrnii*, the "immortal jellyfish," when wounded, sick, or old, can change its cells into young cells again. In theory, it could keep doing this forever.[68] That means if scientists can find the "switch" in human DNA that causes aging, they may be able to slow it down, or even make old cells young again. This is what Wolverine does every time he rapidly heals.

Wolverine is a fictional hero, but Jesus is real. And when He was on Earth, He did miracles to instantly heal people. Jesus had the power of God's Spirit. We may not completely understand how Jesus' miracles were possible, but we can always trust in the very real power of God.

Since the beginning of time, people have been seeking eternal youth. A Spanish explorer named Ponce de León searched years for the Fountain of

Youth. The good news is this: God is more than happy to give you eternal life. The Bible says about God's living water, "Let anyone who is thirsty come. Let anyone who desires drink freely from the water of life" (Revelation 22:17 NLT). And the Lord says, "I will give of the fountain of the water of life freely to him who thirsts" (Revelation 21:6 NKJV).

THOR

45.
Above the Dark World

Ages ago, Bor, Thor's grandfather, fought the wicked Elves of Malekith on the Dark World. Malekith wanted to use the Aether, a powerful Infinity Stone, to send the universe into endless night. But Bor defeated him. Then, thinking Malekith's forces were all dead, Bor hid the Aether on the Dark World. But Malekith and some of his army had survived.

In the present day, ancient worlds began to line up, and doorways opened between them. Jane Foster, Thor's girlfriend, was swept through a doorway into the Dark World. The Aether, turning into a mist, entered her, and Jane woke up back on Earth. When Thor found her and saw she wasn't well, he carried her to Asgard to be healed.

Jane was in awe of the beauty of Valhalla, the capital of Asgard. It was filled with life and light. Standing on a balcony, surrounded by beautiful blossoms, all she could do was whisper, "Wow!"[69]

Valhalla was the Viking idea of heaven, and the

scenes in this movie are how many Christians picture "the city of the living God, the heavenly Jerusalem" (Hebrews 12:22 NKJV). "[The Holy City] shone with the glory of God" and was made of "pure gold, as pure as glass" (Revelation 21:11, 18 NIV).

Malekith, sensing where the Aether had gone, attacked Asgard with his starships. There was a fierce battle with laser cannons and hand weapons blazing light. Malekith caused much damage before he was finally driven out. The amazing thing is, the Bible describes Satan making a similar attack on heaven (Revelation 12:7–9).

Thor and Jane then led Malekith away from Asgard, before he attacked again, and fled to the Dark World. Malekith followed them, captured Jane, and drew the Aether into himself. Then Thor and Malekith battled until the Dark Elf was crushed by his own starship.

Valhalla is beautiful, but the Dark World is a shadowy, lifeless place. A dim star in the sky gives little light to the world below. Jesus described hell as "outer darkness" three times (Matthew 22:13 NKJV), and Jude said that the wicked "are like wandering stars, doomed forever to blackest darkness" (Jude 1:13 NLT). How much better to live in God's light, enjoying eternal life in His heavenly city above.

"For you were once darkness," the Bible says, "but now you are light in the Lord. Walk as children of light" (Ephesians 5:8 NKJV). It should make you happy to know that God has prepared a home in paradise for you, where you'll live forever.

SILVER SURFER

46.
Defeating the Devil

A *Silver Surfer* comic, *The Power and the Prize*,[70] really preached the Gospel to me when I was young. In this story, a demon named Mephisto was boasting how millions of lost souls were being swept into his dark kingdom. But Silver Surfer threatened his plans. The demon decided to lure him to his kingdom, saying, "There shall I bend you to my Satanic will."[71]

Mephisto knew that Silver Surfer had a true love, Shalla-bal, back in Zenn-La. So Mephisto led her to Earth, captured her, then told Silver Surfer that he had her.

When Silver Surfer arrived, Mephisto began his temptations. First, he offered Silver Surfer rooms full of jewels and gold if he'd bow down to him. The Surfer wasn't tempted. Then Mephisto offered him three gorgeous women. Again, he refused. Finally, Mephisto showed him a vast galactic empire and promised he'd make him its king. Again, Silver Surfer resisted.

Then Mephisto threatened to send Shalla-bal back

to Zenn-La if he didn't bow down. Silver Surfer would never see her again. But Shalla-bal cried out, "How can love have meaning—if it costs your very soul?"[72] Her words were inspired by Jesus, who asked, "What do you benefit if you gain the whole world but lose your own soul?" (Matthew 16:26 NLT).

These temptations clearly copied Satan's temptations of Christ. "When the tempter came to Him, he said, 'If You are the Son of God, command that these stones become bread.'" But Jesus refused to yield to this temptation. "Then the devil. . .set Him on the pinnacle of the temple, and said to Him, 'If You are the Son of God, throw Yourself down.'" Jesus once again resisted. "The devil. . .showed Him all the kingdoms of the world and their glory. And he said to Him, 'All these things I will give You if You will fall down and worship me.' Then Jesus said to him, 'Away with you, Satan! For it is written, "You shall worship the Lord your God, and Him only you shall serve"'" (Matthew 4:3, 5–6, 8–11 NKJV).

Jesus proved that it's possible to resist Satan's temptations, no matter how desirable they seem. Paul said, "God is faithful; he will not let you be tempted beyond what you can bear" (1 Corinthians 10:13 NIV).

In the end, Jesus commanded, "Away with you,

Satan!" Silver Surfer cried out, "I defy you, Mephisto! Darkness must ever retreat before the light!"[73] You too can resist the devil. The Bible promises, "Resist the devil, and he will flee from you" (James 4:7 NIV).

X-MEN

47.
False Claims to Be God

According to the movie *X-Men: Apocalypse*, since the beginning of man's civilizations, the super-mutant Apocalypse was worshipped as a god. Every nation that saw him called him by a different name. Apocalypse said, "I've been called many things over many lifetimes—Ra, Krishna, Yahweh."[74]

That's a lie. Yahweh is the personal name of God—the Father of Jesus. Wherever you see the word LORD (in small capital letters) in the Bible, it stands for Yahweh (pronounced: *Yah*-way), God's holy name. These verses from the Holman Christian Standard Bible show this clearly: "Who is God besides Yahweh? And who is a rock? Only our God." And, "I know that Yahweh is great; our Lord is greater than all gods" (Psalm 18:31; 135:5 HCSB).

The Jews wanted to show respect for God, so they never spoke His holy name out loud. Whenever they came to *Yahweh* in the text, they said, "the LORD." They didn't want to break the third commandment:

"You shall not misuse the name of the LORD" (Exodus 20:7 NIV).

The *X-Men* movie says that the Egyptian god, Ra, the Hindu god, Krishna, and the Hebrew God, Yahweh, were all really the mutant Apocalypse. He absorbed the powers of so many other mutants until finally he became immortal. This made him so proud that he began to believe that he was God—the one true God, Yahweh.

In the movie, Apocalypse gathered a team of mutants to destroy mankind and create a new world where everyone worshipped him. Moira told Alex Summers that Apocalypse always had four close followers. Alex said, "Like the Four Horsemen of the Apocalypse. He got that one from the Bible."[75] That's right.

In the end of the movie, Jean Grey, the X-Man, uses her full power and burns Apocalypse to ashes. Well, *so much* for him thinking he was God.

You may be surprised by people claiming to be God. But Jesus warned, "Many will come in My name, saying, 'I am the Christ,' and will deceive many" (Matthew 24:5 NKJV). If people will claim to be Jesus Christ, God's Son, don't be surprised if some also claim to be the LORD Himself.

Paul warned, "If he who comes preaches another

Jesus whom we have not preached, or if you receive a different spirit which you have not received, or a different gospel which you have not accepted—you may well put up with it!" (2 Corinthians 11:4 NKJV). *Don't put up with it!* How do you do that? How do you keep from being deceived? Read your Bible and know what it says.

SPIDER-MAN

48.
Proving You're Ready

In the movie *Captain America: Civil War*, Peter Parker was a fifteen-year-old student from Queens, New York. One day, he had a surprise visit from the famous inventor and superhero Tony Stark (Iron Man). Stark gave Peter a high-tech Spider-Man suit and pulled him to Germany to fight other Avengers.

Afterward, Stark realized he took a real risk bringing a "kid" into battle. So when he got Peter home, he told him, "I know you want to save the world. But. . . you're not ready yet."[76] But Peter now had his heart set on being an Avenger. In the movie *Spider-Man: Homecoming*, he constantly called Stark's office to give him updates on his progress.

Eventually, Peter learned that Stark could find him wherever he goes. He got his friend Ned Leeds to remove the tracker from his suit. That's when they learn that the costume has many powers but Stark had it set on "Baby Monitor" mode. Upset, Peter said, "I'm sick of Mr. Stark treating me like a kid." Ned replied, "But you *are* a kid."[77]

Then one day, Peter made a huge mistake and Iron Man had to rescue him. He then took away Peter's Spider-Man suit, telling him he wasn't ready for it. Peter was crushed.

In the Bible, a young man named John Mark knew what it was like to be treated as immature and "not ready." As a youth, Mark was very talented and seemed to have a promising future. So Barnabas talked the apostle Paul into bringing him on their mission trip as a helper. But several weeks into the trip, Mark decided he didn't like being a bag boy and headed back home (Acts 13:5, 13).

The next time Paul and Barnabas went on a mission trip, "Barnabas. . .wanted to take along John Mark. But Paul disagreed strongly, since John Mark had deserted them in Pamphylia and had not continued with them in their work" (Acts 15:37–38 NLT). It seemed like Mark had washed out big-time. But the good news is, a few years later, Mark had changed and Paul saw he could be depended on. So they worked together again. When Timothy was traveling his way, Paul told him, "Bring Mark with you when you come, for he will be helpful to me in my ministry" (2 Timothy 4:11 NLT).

There will be times when you'll be upset that adults

don't trust you with important responsibility. Like Peter and Mark, you may have to spend more time getting ready, proving that you're mature and ready for the job. It's a process many young people have to go through, so don't sweat it.

ROBOCOP

49.
Programming and Compassion

The 2014 *RoboCop* movie is set in Chicago in 2028, when robot police are being used in most of the world. However, they were forbidden in America. A company named OmniCorp got around this law by putting a man inside a robot. When police detective Alex Murphy is murdered, a doctor put what's left of him inside a machine. Alex moved his robot body with his mind, and Dr. Norton promised him, "You're in control."[78]

That's what he told *Alex*. To OmniCorp he said, "The human element will. . .always interfere with the system."[79] To stop Alex from "interfering," Norton made his mind sleepy. Then the computers took over and made the decisions. This way, they turned him into a deadly fighting machine. However, when Alex's wife tells him about their son's problems, he's moved with concern. He fights against the computer and takes back control of his body.

There's an important lesson here for Christians: it's good to have doctrine—teachings that guide the way you think. After all, the apostles often spoke about the difference between true and false doctrines. But like OmniCorp, religious people make up their *own* teachings—their own programming—to override the commands of God in the Bible.

Dr. Norton said that "compassion. . .will always interfere with the system," and OmniCorp saw this as a problem. So did the Pharisees in Jesus' day. They were always creating doctrines that shut out love and compassion. Jesus scolded them, saying, "You have a fine way of setting aside the commands of God in order to observe your own traditions!" (Mark 7:9 NIV).

The greatest commands are to love God and to love others. John stated that whoever sees a fellow believer in need but shows no compassion doesn't have real faith (1 John 3:17). The Pharisees went through the motions of being righteous but lacked compassion and mercy.

Do you ever do this? Do you allow your mental programming and doctrines and opinions to shut down compassion? If someone asks for your help, is your reaction, "Everyone is responsible to make their *own* way in life"? Or when asked to forgive someone, do you mutter, "I will if they're *truly* sorry"—and then never accept their apology as real?

Of course, you can't help *everyone* who asks you, but if you can, you should consider doing so. Proverbs 3:27 (NKJV) says, "Do not withhold good from those to whom it is due, when it is in the power of your hand to do so."

Override selfish programming today, and allow God's love and compassion to motivate you.

SUPERMAN
50.
On Earth for a Reason

When Superman was just a baby, his world, Krypton, was about to explode. His father, Jor-El, couldn't escape, but he wanted to save his son. Therefore he sent him to Earth in a small spaceship, and it landed in a farm field in Kansas. Jonathan and Martha Kent found it and raised the baby as their own son, calling him Clark Kent.

Earth has weaker gravity than Krypton. Plus, it has a yellow sun, while Krypton's sun is red. So growing up on Earth gave Clark extraordinary powers. His father, Jor-El, knew this would happen and said, "He'll be a god to them."[80] Sure enough, Clark began to develop superhuman strength.

Clark didn't feel special. He was afraid of his strange powers—like being able to see through things. Plus, because he was different, bullies picked on him. But his father warned him not to use his strength, even to defend himself. Jesus also could have used His powers to protect Himself, but He didn't (John 18:3–6).

Talking about Jonathan Kent, Clark said, "My father

believed that if the world found out who I really was, they'd reject me. . .out of fear."[81] For a long time, Clark traveled around, quietly doing good and saving lives—just like Jesus did when He was on Earth. But, like Jesus, Clark was destined to become a shining light to all mankind.

The parallel between Superman being sent to Earth by his father, Jor-El, and Jesus being sent to Earth by His Father is clear. And Superman's mother on Krypton could have been describing Jesus' destiny when she predicted the future of her son. She said, "He will be an outcast. They'll kill him."[82] The apostle Peter told the people of Jerusalem that this is what they had done to Jesus: "You nailed him to a cross and killed him" (Acts 2:23 NLT).

But the good news is, "God. . .raised him back to life" (Acts 2:24 NLT). The movie makers also had Superman come back to life after he died.

Jesus said, "I am the light of the world" (John 8:12 NLT), and if His Spirit dwells in you, then you become a shining light to show others the way. Jesus said, "You are the light of the world. . . . Let your good deeds shine out for all to see" (Matthew 5:14, 16 NLT).

You can also expect to be misunderstood and rejected at times—just like Jesus was. And like Clark Kent, you might be unknown and your good deeds largely unseen, but don't be discouraged: you have a great destiny. You too were sent to Earth for a reason.

BATMAN
51.
Don't Fear Scarecrows

The movie *Batman Begins* shows Bruce Wayne as a young boy, falling into a dry well. Hundreds of bats flew around him, so for many years afterward, he was terrified of bats. Not long after, his parents were killed by a robber, right in front of him. This also caused Bruce great fear. When he grew up, he traveled the world to learn how to conquer his fears. He ended up in the Himalayas where Ra's al Ghul trained him. Bruce not only mastered his fears, but he also learned fighting skills.

One day, however, he found out that Ra's al Ghul planned to destroy Gotham, Bruce's city, because it had so much crime. Bruce returned to Gotham to fight the criminals and save the city. He feared bats, so he created a Batman costume and legend to strike fear into the hearts of his foes.

Bruce discovered that Dr. Crane (Scarecrow) was working for Ra's al Ghul and had put chemicals in Gotham's water supply. The chemicals would cause everyone to be filled with fear, go insane, and destroy the city. Fortunately, Batman stopped them in time.

This movie's plot is like actual terror plots in the world. Small groups of men plan to bomb a public place or to attack crowds with other weapons. But killing a few people isn't their main goal. Their *main* goal is to cause people to fear so they give up.

You probably haven't been attacked by terrorists, but you may be tempted to fear bad kids at school. Often, your fears are just that—only fear—and there's not really much of a threat. In the movie, Dr. Crane used a scarecrow mask to frighten people. In reality, a scarecrow can't do anything. It just *looks* scary. It *appears* to be alive to scare crows away. You're smarter than a crow, so don't fear the scarecrows of this world.

The Bible says, "There is no fear in love; but perfect love casts out fear" (1 John 4:18 NKJV). If you feel fear, know that it's not from God. "God has not given us a spirit of fear, but of power and of love and of a sound mind" (2 Timothy 1:7 NKJV). How can you have a sound mind, free from fear? How can you experience power in the face of danger? By trusting God.

Once when David was seized by Philistines who wanted to kill him, he was afraid. But he believed God would protect him, so he said, "When I am afraid, I will put my trust in You" (Psalm 56:3 NASB). That's what you must do also.

CATWOMAN
52.
Beauty Is Skin Deep

In comicbooks and movies, many superheroines wear costumes that are little more than bikinis. And even movies that show them in full-body costumes reveal every curve. Now, there's nothing wrong with actresses being attractive. But the movie *Catwoman* took this too far. The movie was about a courageous woman risking her life to expose a criminal beauty industry—yet it contradicted itself by constantly focusing on Catwoman's body and beauty.

In *Catwoman*, Patience Phillips worked for a cosmetics company that made skin cream that helps people stop aging. But Patience overheard company leaders talk about the horrible health risks of using their cream. When they realized Patience had heard them, they sent guards to kill her. Then, as she lay dead, a Mau cat, sent by an Egyptian goddess, appeared. It brought Patience back to life and gave her power to fight. She then set out as Catwoman to expose the company.

The movie *Fantastic Four* started off right, showing Susan Storm (Invisible Woman) trying to restart a romance with the man she loved, Reed Richards. In the end, Reed proposed to her and she accepted. It was a truly biblical ending to their love.

But the movie producers seemed obsessed with Invisible Woman needing to disappear but her regular clothing not vanishing. How could they solve this? Simple. They had her remove all her clothes. She did this *twice* in the first movie and again in the second movie. The first time, her brother Johnny groaned, "This is so *wrong*,"[83] and the second time, Sue asked, "*Why* does this always happen to me?"[84] By the third time, viewers were asking the same thing.

The answer is that the movie producers thought that by tempting viewers with glimpses of Sue Storm's body, they would bring more viewers to watch their movies. But the movies did poorly in the theaters anyway. They would have been better off leaving those scenes out of the movies.

Now, God created physical beauty to attract men and women to each another. One love song tells a princess that "the King will greatly desire your beauty" (Psalm 45:11 NKJV). But God made this special desire and love to be enjoyed in marriage. In the end of the second *Fantastic Four* movie, Sue and Reed were married and promised to be faithful to each other.

Remember, though, physical beauty is only skin deep. Or, as the Bible says, "Beauty does not last; but a woman who fears the LORD will be greatly praised" (Proverbs 31:30 NLT). So seek to love God and have a beautiful spirit.

BATMAN

53.
Decent Men in an Indecent Time

In the movie *Batman: The Dark Knight*, a villain called the Joker seems to be the star of the film—not Batman. The Joker always seems in control, is fearless, and constantly keeps one step ahead of his foes. He's always outwitting Batman (Bruce Wayne), who scrambles to keep up. That's an odd switch.

Everything goes wrong for the good guys. Bruce's girlfriend, Rachel, rejects him to marry Harvey Dent, a powerful lawyer whom Bruce respects. Then Rachel is murdered. Then Harvey is burned so badly that he turns away from good and becomes a villain. Then he dies.

The producers were trying to make a "darker, more realistic" movie—and they certainly made it darker. They even made Batman cruel. A "realistic" approach had worked in the first film. But following this path in the second movie took viewers to a *much* darker place.

It's true that the Bible also describes the dark sides and unheroic actions of good men. King David, for example, usually loved God passionately, stood up for what was right, showed mercy to his enemies, and wrote inspired worship songs. Yet he gave in to his selfish, dark side and had one of his loyal soldiers killed so he could take his wife.

Batman admires Harvey Dent, calling him the "White Knight." Harvey is a courageous, good lawyer who wants to help people. But the Joker changes him. He badly burns him, driving him insane, until he becomes evil.

A decent person is someone who is respectable and good, and who treats others fairly and honestly. Harvey told Batman, "You thought we could be decent men in an indecent time! But you were wrong. The world is cruel."[85] Yes, the world *can* be cruel. Make no mistake about it. But the Bible says, "Be not overcome of evil, but overcome evil with good" (Romans 12:21 KJV).

God's Word also states, "Live clean, innocent lives... shining like bright lights in a world full of crooked and perverse people" (Philippians 2:15 NLT).

With God's help, you can rise above the darkness. You don't have to become bitter when you suffer. The apostle Peter said to remember Jesus' example: "When they hurled their insults at him, he did not retaliate; when he suffered, he made no threats" (1 Peter 2:23

NIV). Yes, difficult as it may be, you can follow Jesus' example. "Think of what he went through; how he put up with so much hatred from sinners!" (Hebrews 12:3 GNT). It may look like you're losing, but God will see to it that you're rewarded in the end.

GREEN LANTERN
54.
Chosen to Wear the Ring

There's more than one Green Lantern. There's a whole police force of them from many planets. All Green Lanterns wear a ring with powerful energy. It lets them create whatever they imagine.

Long ago, their leaders sent a ring to each part of the universe, where the rings chose their bearers. A ring bearer had to be without fear. In the movie, the Green Lantern Abin Sur was attacked by a supervillain. He crashed on Earth, and knowing he was dying, he sent his ring to find a new Green Lantern. The ring chose Hal Jordan.

Later, Hal went to the planet Oa and trained to use the ring. There, an alien saw that Hal had fear and told him he was unworthy of his ring. But another Green Lantern said, "The ring never makes a mistake." Hal replied, "This time it did."[86] However, a friend assured Hal that though he wasn't fearless, he was able to *overcome* fear.[87] And he did.

What are *you* afraid of? Know this: with God's help,

you can conquer your fears and go on to do amazing things. Don't worry. God will be with you and not forsake you.

In biblical times, kings wore rings with special designs on them. They were called "signet" rings and were used to "sign" royal laws and commands. After an order was written on a tablet, the king pressed his ring in the clay. When he favored someone, he let them use his ring. King Xerxes handed his ring to Mordecai. He told him to write a law and seal it with his ring (Esther 8:2, 8).

God even compared people to rings. He told one ruler, "I will. . .make you like a signet ring; for I have chosen you" (Haggai 2:23 NKJV). But even if God *has* chosen you for a job, if you fail to do that job, you can lose your position (Jeremiah 22:24).

If the Lord has given you some task to do, make sure you *do* it. It's okay if you're nervous and make mistakes. Everyone messes up, so don't doubt that you're the right person for the job. But the important thing is this: Do you stick to your job and not give up? Are you faithful to do it even when you're afraid or when you're bored and it's no longer fun?

If you give up, someone else will take over your

work and finish it—and get the reward God had meant for you. So be faithful and fulfill your calling. Don't lose your glorious reward. It's worth fighting for.

SHAZAM

55.
Instant Power

In the *Shazam* comics, a boy named Billy Batson shouts, "Shazam!" and is struck by a bolt of lightning. This transforms him into an adult superhero. He used to be called Captain Marvel but is now called Shazam.

Shazam comes from the first letters of the names of those who give Billy power: **S**olomon, **H**ercules, **At**las, **Z**eus, **A**chilles, and **M**ercury. Billy has vast wisdom like Solomon. Hercules gives him super-strength. Atlas grants him endurance. Zeus helps him resist magical attacks. Achilles gives him courage and fighting skills. And Mercury lets him fly and run at great speed.

Many people wish that they *could* just shout one word and instantly receive all the wisdom, power, and courage they need to face life's problems. God *does* make a great change in your life when Jesus enters your heart. The Bible says, "If anyone is in Christ, he is a new creation. . .all things have become new" (2 Corinthians 5:17 NKJV). But the *full* transformation takes a lifetime and means being daily changed and renewed by God's Spirit.

Shazam dwells in a refuge called the Rock of Eternity, and he's one with the Rock—so much so that he can only be away from it for twenty-four hours at a time. God is *our* Rock of Eternity. The Bible says, "The LORD is my rock and my fortress," and, "The LORD has been my defense, and my God the rock of my refuge" (Psalm 18:2; 94:22 NKJV). You too shouldn't go long without spending time with God in prayer.

Just as Shazam is one with the Rock of Eternity, Christians are one with God. "He who is joined to the Lord is one spirit with Him" (1 Corinthians 6:17 NKJV). If you're a believer, the Spirit of Christ lives in your heart. Jesus lives in *you*, but you must also live in *Him*.

It's ironic that Achilles is one of the heroes helping Shazam, because Achilles had a famous weakness. He had a weak heel, so an "Achilles' heel" is a weakness that can lead to a person's defeat. Shazam's weakness was that he was a proud teenager. If God has given you abilities or talents, be aware of weaknesses that could bring you down. An ancient proverb says, "Know yourself." That means to know what your strengths are. It also means to be aware of your weaknesses and to guard against them.

Then, very importantly, make sure you "know the LORD" (Hosea 6:3 KJV). He alone can strengthen your spirit, steel your will, and help you overcome. "The people who know their God will be strong" (Daniel 11:32 HCSB).

JOKER
56.
Beware Evil Heroes

The Joker has been a clever criminal for a while. In *Batman: The Dark Knight* he was insane and cruel, but somehow very "cool." He then went from a villain to a dark hero in *Suicide Squad*.

Showing evil "heroes" is a growing trend, but it's not the first time we've seen this. The Comics Code talked about this back in the 1950s. Point 5 stated that criminals shouldn't be shown to be so cool that you want to copy them. But in recent years, most comic-books publishers abandoned the Code. They were tired of heroes who were always good and villains who were always bad. So they began creating cruel heroes and likable villains.

The movie *The Suicide Squad* starred DC Comics' worst villains. In the film, a secret government agency created Task Force X, made up of the worst of the worst. They then sent them on dangerous missions in exchange for fewer years in prison. Their missions were so dangerous they were called "The Suicide Squad."

A number of soldiers in past wars were criminals. Some received another chance after they did acts of heroism, but others proved they were completely evil by doing war crimes. The Suicide Squad is like some of David's men. When he was being hunted by King Saul, many noble warriors joined him. But several lowlifes also came. "Then others began coming—men who were in trouble or in debt or who were just discontented" (1 Samuel 22:2 NLT). A later verse describes "evil trouble-makers" who followed David (1 Samuel 30:22 NLT).

David later realized that such warriors were no help, so he sent them away, saying, "I hate all who deal crookedly; I will have nothing to do with them. . . . I will not allow deceivers to serve in my house" (Psalm 101:3, 7 NLT).

Movies like *Suicide Squad* leave viewers confused: They enjoy the realistic acting, the interesting plot, the special effects, and the action. But it leaves a bad taste in their mouth when movies make evil people look cool. The Bible tells us, "Do not imitate what is evil but what is good" (3 John 1:11 NIV), adding, "Remember your leaders, who spoke the word of God to you. . . . Imitate their faith" (Hebrews 13:7 NIV).

You must be sensitive to God when He tells you that certain movies, books, or video games are "off."

David stated that he refused to look at anything vile and worthless. He would reject sick ideas and stay away from every evil (Psalm 101:3–4). *Suicide Squad* is an example of an evil that you should stay away from.

BATMAN AND SUPERMAN
57.
Hope and Justice

The movie *Batman vs. Superman: Dawn of Justice* shows Batman still bitter over his parents' murders, many years later. Plus, he's angry that several of his (Bruce Wayne's) workers died during Superman's recent battle with Zog.

This movie is called *Dawn of Justice*, but having lost all faith in justice, the once-noble Batman turns into a vigilante. He becomes so cruel that he begins marking his enemies with a burning brand. Batman even makes a spear to kill Superman. He argues that even if there is a small chance that Superman is a threat, he will destroy him. He even fights a villain to get the Kryptonite to kill Superman with.

Whatever happened to Batman, the superhero? Batman was once famous for fighting evil criminals. No wonder Superman complained, "No one stays good in this world."[88] When good people give up hope, they become suspicious. Then they judge others. Then they become merciless.

In this sad movie, Batman said, "I bet your parents taught you that you mean something, that you're here for a reason. My parents taught me a different lesson, dying in the gutter for no reason at all."[89] He was saying that life is cruel and has no meaning or hope.

Batman was wrong. You *do* mean something, and you *are* here for a reason. Life isn't just a bunch of senseless pain and grief. God knows His people will suffer problems, accidents, and injustice. Yet the apostle Paul said, "In all these things we are more than conquerors through Him who loved us" (Romans 8:37 NKJV). Even when you seem to be losing, victory will one day be yours. Even when this life isn't fair, know that God will judge everything in the next life. So if you're suffering, keep trusting God. He sees and He cares.

It's exciting to see Batman slugging it out with Superman. It's quite the fight. But it makes you wonder, with so many villains around, why the moviemakers had the good guys fight *each other*. But good friends *do* have arguments. Misunderstandings happen; people say and do thoughtless things; and those they hurt often *do* refuse to forgive.

It takes Superman sacrificing himself to destroy Doomsday, for Batman to wake up. After the Man of

Steel died, Batman confessed to Wonder Woman, "I've failed him."[90] How had he failed him? By being filled with anger and suspicion. He was so set against Superman that he believed anything negative about him. And once he was convinced that Superman was a threat, he felt that he was right to try to kill him.

May you *never* give up hope in justice or judge others quickly.

WONDER WOMAN
58.
Amazons of God

Diana Prince (Wonder Woman) is daughter of the god Zeus and Queen Hippolyta of the Amazons. Zeus created the Amazons then placed them on the hidden island of Themyscira. In 1918, near the end of the First World War, Steve Trevor crashed his plane there. Diana then returned to London with him to help stop the war.

It was thrilling to see Diana in action in the movie *Wonder Woman*. In addition to her powers, she has amazing weapons. Anyone roped by her lasso, the Lariat of Hestia, is forced to tell the truth. She also has a pair of bracelets that she uses to shield herself from bullets. Wonder Woman has long been the greatest comicbook heroine.

The Bible has mighty women as well. Deborah was judge of Israel in an age when men usually ruled. But she had such great wisdom that men came from far and wide to seek her advice (Judges 4:4–5).

At that time, powerful Canaanite armies, led by General Sisera, were crushing Israel. So Deborah told the warrior Barak to gather an army. God would help him defeat Sisera. Barak said, "I will go, but only if you go with me." Deborah replied, "Very well. . . . But you will receive no honor in this venture, for the LORD's victory over Sisera will be at the hands of a woman" (Judges 4:8–9 NLT).

Barak was willing to send his men against a powerful army, but he wanted to be sure that God was with them. If Deborah being with him guaranteed success, Barak didn't mind that a woman got some credit for winning the battle. Many men could learn from this attitude. Christians know that "there is no longer. . . male and female. For you are all one in Christ Jesus" (Galatians 3:28 NLT). God can use women as much as He can use men.

However, women, like men, can become discouraged. Diana had believed that all she needed to do was kill the evil god Ares and all the fighting would end. She didn't understand that *people* caused wars too. She became disappointed by how selfish and violent people were. At the end of the war, she became discouraged. She said, "A hundred years ago I walked away from mankind."[91]

When you're young and full of idealism, you often do great, daring things. But you also make mistakes and are misunderstood. And people fail you. You may back off for some time. It's good to learn from your mistakes and to know that people are only human, but don't withdraw from them forever. People still need heroes and heroines who can rise up and do great things.

FLASH

59.
Running the Race

Flash is one of DC Comics' most famous superheroes. The man behind the mask is Barry Allen. He works in a police crime lab and gained his powers when he was accidentally covered with chemicals and struck by lightning. After that, he found he could run at super-speed.

Marvel Comics also has a speedy superhero, Quicksilver. In the movie *Days of Future Past*, he showed what lightning-fast people can do. They can push bullets to the side so they miss targets. They can check people's ID so quickly that the people don't even know they've moved. Would you like to be so fast no one can stop you? You'd better use such speed for good! The Flash did, but at first, Quicksilver often used it to steal things.

There were many speedy men in the Bible. The swiftest were chosen as runners to carry important news, especially after battles (2 Samuel 18:19–32). And "Asahel. . .could run as fast as a wild deer" (2 Samuel 2:18 GNT).

There was also a normal man who once was super speedy. God did a miracle to help the prophet Elijah run faster than a chariot. "The power of the LORD came on Elijah and. . .he ran ahead of Ahab all the way to Jezreel" (1 Kings 18:46 NIV). That was a *long* run too! It began at Mount Carmel, thirty miles away from Jezreel.

But being fast isn't enough. The Bible gives other keys to success. First, it says, "Let us strip off every weight that slows us down, especially the sin that so easily trips us up. And let us run with endurance the race God has set before us" (Hebrews 12:1 NLT). Sin and bad habits weigh you down, so ditch them.

Second: Racecourses are clearly marked out, and to win you have to stay inside the lines. You can't run out of bounds. "Athletes cannot win the prize unless they follow the rules" (2 Timothy 2:5 NLT). In life, people commonly cheat to get ahead, but Christians must follow the rules.

Third: You have to persevere. You have to keep at it. You can't stop by the side of the road and fall asleep. At the end of his life of faithful service to God, Paul was able to say, "I have fought the good fight, I have finished the race, I have kept the faith" (2 Timothy 4:7

NIV). Being fast is good, but you have to actually cross the finish line.

The Bible says, "Run in such a way as to get the prize" (1 Corinthians 9:24 NIV). Are you doing that?

60.
Are You a True Believer?

Why do people have such a love for superheroes? Why do they flock by the millions to see the latest superhero movies? Sure, the films are action packed and have astonishing special effects, but there are other reasons. The main one is that they meet a deep need.

People fear many things today. They want someone to protect them. This is why believers pray for angels to stand guard around them. The Bible states that "angels. . .are stronger and more powerful" than humans, and promises, "The angel of the LORD. . .delivers them" (2 Peter 2:11; Psalm 34:7 NIV).

Many things in the world seem out of control—at least, out of *your* control—and you long for a hero to stand between you and the evil and save you. You wait for a powerful Savior to deliver you from your problems and bitter enemies. And the good news is this: God has sent the Savior—His Son, Jesus—and He comes to rescue you. He not only saves you from death in hell but also from danger in this life now.

Are you a true believer? "Anyone who believes in

God's Son has eternal life" and "he is able, once and forever, to save those who come to God through him" (John 3:36; Hebrews 7:25 NLT). If you believe that Jesus died on the cross for your sins and rose from the dead, you're saved. God then sends His Spirit into your heart (Galatians 4:6), and He will never leave or forsake you.

Have you put your faith in Jesus Christ? If you're not sure, you can pray a prayer like this: "Dear God, I believe that Jesus is Your Son, that He died on the cross to pay the penalty for my sins. I believe that He was buried and raised from the dead. I ask You now to forgive my sins and to send your Spirit into my heart. Give me the strength to obey You. In Jesus' name, I pray. Amen."

Once you're a true believer, then you too can be heroic. You probably won't have superpowers, but you can have courage, perseverance, and self-sacrifice. Aunt May said about Spider-Man, "[We] need a hero—courageous, self-sacrificing people, setting examples for all of us."[92]

You may not *feel* like a hero, but neither did most of the men and women God used down through history. But they loved God and others and were faithful. Then, one day when they weren't even expecting anything special, something happened, they stepped up to help—and they were transformed into a hero. God can use you too!

END NOTES

[1] Fantastic Four #72, March 1968

[2] Dr. Strange issue 13, April 1976

[3] The Mighty Thor Annual #14, November 1989

[4] Warlock Chronicles #2, August 1993

[5] The movie, *Captain America: The First Avenger* (2011)

[6] The movie, *The Avengers* (2012)

[7] The Ultimates 2 Volume 1: Gods and Monsters (2005)

[8] The movie, *Avengers: Age of Ultron* (2015)

[9] The movie, *Spider-Man* (2002)

[10] The movie, *The Avengers* (2012)

[11] The movie, *Iron Man 3* (2013)

[12] Ibid.

[13] The movie, *The Avengers* (2012)

[14] Ibid.

[15] The movie, *Thor: The Dark World* (2013)

[16] The movie, *Captain America: The Winter Soldier* (2014)

[17] Ibid.

[18] The movie, *The Avengers* (2012)

[19] The movie, *Iron Man 2* (2010)

[20] Ibid.

[21] Ibid.

[22] The movie, *Avengers: Age of Ultron* (2015)

[23] The movie, *Ant-Man* (2015)

[24] The movie, *Avengers: Age of Ultron* (2015)

[25] The movie, *X-Men: The Last Stand* (2006)

[26] The movie, *X-Men* (2000)

[27] Ibid.

[28] Ibid.

[29] The movie, *X-Men: The Last Stand* (2006)

[30] Ibid.

[31] Ibid.

[32] Ibid.

[33] The movie, *X-Men* (2000)

[34] The movie, *X2: X-Men United* (2003)

[35] The movie, *X-Men* (2000)

[36] Ibid.

[37] The movie, *X-Men: The Last Stand* (2006)

[38] The movie, *X2: X-Men United* (2003)

[39] The movie, *X-Men: The Last Stand* (2006)

[40] The movie, *X-Men* (2000)

[41] The movie, *Captain America: Civil War* (2016)

[42] The movie, *Batman Begins* (2005)

[43] The movie, *Spider-Man 3* (2007)

[44] The movie, *Fantastic Four: The Rise of the Silver Surfer* (2007)

[45] The movie, *Fantastic Four* (2005)

[46] The movie, *Fantastic Four* (2005)

[47] Ibid.

[48] The movie, *Fantastic Four* (2005)

[49] Fantastic Four, Vol. 3, No. 56 (August, 2002)

[50] The movie, *Fantastic Four* (2005)

[51] Silver Surfer, vol. 1, no. 1 (August, 1968)

[52] Silver Surfer, vol. 1, no. 3 (December, 1968)

[53] The movie, *Iron Man 3* (2013)

[54] The movie, *X-Men Origins: Wolverine* (2009)

[55] Ibid.

[56] The movie, *Guardians of the Galaxy* (2014)

[57] The movie, *Deadpool* (2016)

[58] Ibid.

[59] The Ultimates 2 Volume 1: Gods and Monsters (2005)

[60] The movie, *Daredevil* (2003)

[61] The Amazing Spider-Man, vol. 2, issue no. 46, pgs. 6–8 (December, 2002)

[62] The Amazing Spider-Man, vol. 2, issue no. 53, page 6 (July, 2003)

[63] The movie, *X-Men* (2000)

[64] Ibid.

[65] The movie, *The Avengers* (2012)

[66] Ibid.

[67] The movie, *Avengers: Age of Ultron* (2015)

[68] As reported in the January 2009 issue of National Geographic

[69] The movie, *Thor: The Dark World* (2013)

[70] Silver Surfer, vol. 1, no. 3 (December, 1968)

[71] Ibid.

[72] Ibid.

[73] Ibid.

[74] The movie trailer, *X-Men: Apocalypse* (2016)

[75] Ibid.

[76] The movie, *Spider-Man: Homecoming* (2017); trailer

[77] The movie, *Spider-Man: Homecoming* (2017)

[78] The movie, *RoboCop* (2014)

[79] Ibid.

[80] The movie, *Man of Steel* (2013)

[81] Ibid.

[82] Ibid.

[83] The movie, *Fantastic Four* (2005)

[84] Ibid.

[85] The movie, *Batman: The Dark Knight* (2008)

[86] The movie, *Green Lantern* (2011)

[87] Ibid.

[88] The movie, *Batman vs. Superman: Dawn of Justice* (2016)

[89] Ibid.

[90] Ibid.

[91] The movie, *Batman vs. Superman: Dawn of Justice* (2016)

[92] The movie, *Spider-Man 2* (2004)

ABOUT THE AUTHOR

Ed Strauss was a freelance writer living in British Columbia, Canada, who passed into heaven in 2018. He authored or coauthored more than fifty books for children, tweens, and adults. Ed had a passion for biblical apologetics and besides writing for Barbour, he was also published by Zondervan, Tyndale, Moody, and Focus on the Family. Ed has three children: Sharon, Daniel, and Michelle Strauss.